PRAISE FOR MICHELLE JOY LEVINE

"... one of a kind ... jargon free ... richly informative book about why people need to overeat ... an appetizing scholarly treat while we learn ... what makes us tick and ... want to eat to excess."
— Monica Rawn, C.S.W., B.C.D., Psychoanalyst; Psychotherapist; Faculty, Training and Control Analyst, Vice President SPSR; Training and Control Analyst, New York Freudian Society; Member, International Psychoanalytic Association.

"... quite brilliant ... innovative ... a tremendous accomplishment ... extremely useful for ... [those] struggling with problems of overeating ... fascinating insight into unconscious factors interfering with ... weight reduction."
— Morton Kissen, Ph.D., Psychoanalyst; Professor, Psychology, Doctoral and Postdoctoral, Adelphi University; Author of *Affect, Object and Character Structure,* and *Gender and Psychoanalytic Treatment.*

"... unique and powerful ... join[s] with the reader in a real and deep way ... vivid and relevant case examples ... I highly recommend this important book."
— Susan Sherman, D.S.W., Psychotherapist; Adjunct faculty, Adelphi University, School of Social Work.

"At long last those of us who have an unhealthy relationship with food can understand why ... a must read for ... those who professionally treat ... or are themselves overweight."
— Annette Mont, C.S.W., Psychotherapist and Lecturer.

"I highly recommend this book to therapists as well as the general reader ... As a clinician treating eating disorders for 24 years ... this is one of the best ... conveys ideas in a simple but powerful manner."
— Sheila Baum, C.S.W., Psychotherapist.

D0107079

I Wish I Were Thin

I wish I were fat

The Real Reasons We Overeat And What We Can Do About It

Michelle Joy Levine

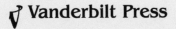 Vanderbilt Press

First Edition

Library of Congress Catalog Card Number: 97-060106

ISBN 0-9656686-4-9

Manufactured in the United States of America

10 9 8 7 6 5 4 3 2 1

Includes Endnotes, Glossary, Bibliography and Index

The author is grateful for permission to reprint the following:

Reprinted by permission of *FORBES FYI* Magazine © Forbes Inc., 1996 "I'm Not Half The Man I Used To Be," by Anthony Brandt.

Reprinted by permission of Harold Ober Associates, Incorporated, *The Fifty Minute Hour,* © 1954 by Robert Linder.

Reprinted by permission of University of Chicago Press, excerpts from *Complete Greek Tragedies* Vol. I by David Grene and Richmond Lattimore, eds. Copyright © 1960 by Richmond Lattimore.

Reprinted by permission of St. Martin's Press Incorporated, *OPRAH!* by Robert Waldron Copyright © 1987 by Robert Waldron.

Reprinted by permission of George Braziller, Inc., *Masochism: An Interpretation of Coldness and Cruelty* by Gilles Deleuze. Copyright © 1971 by Gilles DeLeuze.

Reprinted with permission of Simon & Schuster, *The Snow White Syndrome: All about Envy* by Betsy Cohen. Copyright © 1986 by Betsy Cohen.

Reprinted with the permission of Simon & Schuster from *Lady Oracle* by Margaret Atwood. Copyright © 1976 by Margaret Atwood.

Reprinted with the permission of Westminster John Knox Press from *Cinderella and Her Sisters: The Envied and the Envying* by Ann and Barry Ulanov. Copyright © 1983 by Ann and Barry Ulanov.

Reprinted by permission of Harper Collins Publishers from *The Interpretation of Dreams* by Sigmund Freud. Translated from the German and edited by James Strachey. Published in the United States by Basic Books, Inc., 1956 by arrangement with George Allen & Unwin, Ltd. and the Hogarth Press, Ltd.

Reprinted by permission of the *International Journal of Psychoanalysis,* "The Golden Fantasy: A Regressive Reaction To Separation Anxiety," by Sydney Smith 1977, 58, 311.

Reprinted by permission of Harper & Collins, Publishers, Inc. from *Roseanne, My Life As A Woman* by Roseanne Barr. Copyright © 1989 by Roseanne Barr.

Reprinted by permission of W.W. Norton & Company. Inc. from *SUCH A PRETTY FACE: Being Fat in America* by Marcia Millman. Copyright © 1980 by Marcia Millman.

Reprinted by permission of The Putnam Publishing Group from *MY LIFE ON A DIET* By Rene Taylor. Copyright © 1986 by Rene Taylor.

Reprinted by permission of Bantam Books, a division of Bantam, Doubleday, Dell Publishing Group, Inc. from *The James Coco Diet* by James Coco. Copyright © 1984 by James Coco.

Reprinted by permission of Waverly, Williams & Williams, "The Occurrence and Meaning Of Dreams of Food and Eating," by Walter W. Hamburger, M.D., in *PSYCHOSOMATIC MEDICINE,* 1958, Vol. XX (1):13.

Reprinted by permission of Breaking Free, *Feeding The Hungry Heart,* by Geneen Roth, Copyright © 1977 Geneen Roth.

To Len and Diane, on whose nurturance I can always depend

and

To the memory of my Mother

Table of Contents

Part Three
TO BE OR NOT TO BE, THAT IS THE QUESTION

Part Four
OEDIPUS REX

Part Five
THE EVIL EYE

Part Six
FAILING TO EAT OR EATING TO FAIL—MASOCHISM

Part Seven
THOSE EATING-MY-HEART-OUT-BLUES

Part Eight
SMORGASBORD

Part Nine
FURTHERMORE . . .

Acknowledgments

Writing a book about our need for nurturance causes me to especially value and appreciate all the caring and nurturance I have received from so many people who assisted me while writing this book. I recognize how fortunate I am to have all these loving people in my life.

For spending countless hours reading, rereading, editing and reediting numerous versions of my manuscript, I am deeply indebted to Len Troupp. Without his intelligent, objective perspective and continued patience, faith and caring, I could not have fulfilled my dream of writing this book. I am extremely grateful to Diane Fero, for reading and editing countless versions of this manuscript and for offering her poignant poems that appear in this book. I am deeply thankful to her for her continuous, enthusiastic encouragement and love.

I am truly grateful to Dr. Susan Sherman who, despite her busy schedule, edited my manuscript, provided invaluable critiques, and offered her overwhelming encouragement. To Dr. Judith Davis I am also indebted for taking time out of her very active agenda to read, edit and provide me with excellent commentary and wonderful support. I am genuinely appreciative of Annette Mont, C.S.W., for reading, editing and offering wonderful and astute critiques of my manuscript. I am deeply grateful to Laurel Guillen, who in the midst of the most busy time of her life, read and edited my book, offering valuable assistance and wonderful encouragement. I am truly thankful to Mary Freedman for reading, editing and offering me invaluable comments about my manuscript. I am also thankful to Mary for making my day, when she called to offer her appraisal of my manuscript, and began with the greeting, "Author, Author!" I am deeply grateful to Sheila Baum, C.S.W., for reading, editing and providing wonderful encouragement and feedback. I am very thankful to Patsy Turrini, A.C.S.W., B.C.D. for editing the book's glossary.

My special thanks to Barbara Aragon, R.N., Judy Blum, Joyce Edward, A.C.S.W., Sheila Felberbaum, C.S.W., R.N., Barbara Fendel, C.S.W., Arline M. Glassel, C.S.W., Arthur M. Goldweber, Ph.D., Laurie Holman, Ph.D., Jeanine Klein, C.S.W., Mort Kissen, Ph.D., Monica Rawn, C.S.W., Fred Sherman, M.D., Helen Steinberg, C.S.W., Bea Weinstein, Ph.D. for reading my manuscript and offering me their feedback and encouragement.

I am appreciative of Joyce Engelson, who offered me her invaluable critique of a previous version of this book. Joan Tassa did a wonderful job proofreading this manuscript and I am very thankful for her help. Maryweld Luhrs did a fine job copy editing the cover of this book, and I am truly grateful to her. I am thankful to Howard Fero who served as a great research assistant. I am grateful to Bill Sommer for his time and sound advice.

To my patients and all those individuals with whom I have been privileged to work and who assisted me in understanding why people overeat, I offer my sincere gratitude. I also express my appreciation to all the talented authors, psychiatrists, psychologists, social workers, and researchers who studied and wrote about child development, psychopathology, and overeating.

Preface

Growing up in a family in which my mother and her siblings were obese started me wondering why my family could not lose weight and look more like my friends' families. I do not remember feeling ashamed of my mother's appearance, but I know I felt very sorry for her. Her appearance shaped her entire existence. My mother declined social invitations and other opportunities because she was so self-conscious about her body.

As for myself, I have been on and off diets since I was a very young girl. My mother put me on diets then fearing I would grow up to be as fat and unhappy as she.

Presently, I am a psychotherapist and psychoanalyst in practice for over twenty years. I have worked with many overweight people, some of whose cases are elaborated in this book. I decided to write this book to convey to the general public the <u>real</u> reasons we overeat, reasons that have not been discussed before.

It is remarkable, with all the diet and fitness books that abound, most people who consistently overeat are not aware of the reasons they do. Despite our recognition that being overweight is dangerous to our health, despite our desire to look the way Madison Avenue and Hollywood suggest, millions of people struggle, albeit unsuccessfully, to lose the weight they wish.

Incredulous as it may sound, although most overeaters desperately wish to be thin, on another level, an unconscious level, they wish to be fat or fear being thin. That is the reason most diets fail and why we often regain any weight we lose. Only by understanding <u>why</u> we unconsciously wish to be fat or fear being thin, can we resolve that wish and finally fulfill our conscious wish to be thin.

The real reasons we overeat may be surprising, but will surely strike home, as you identify with the case histories of people whom I have treated. I wrote this book to help those who suffer from being overweight understand why they overeat, so that ultimately they can be in control over their eating and, therefore, their body appearance and health.

This book will definitely help you understand the particular reasons why you overeat. Once you gain understanding of the specific reasons you overeat, you can follow the 10 minute exercises provided to assist you to finally conquer your desire to overeat.

Part One

Food for Thought

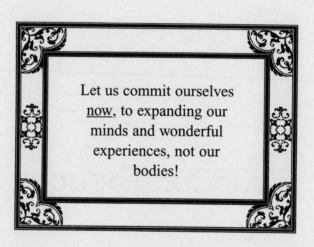

Let us commit ourselves <u>now</u>, to expanding our minds and wonderful experiences, not our bodies!

One

Food For Thought

I have been on a diet for as long as I can remember, at least since I was five years old. My mother put me on a diet then because she said I was getting too fat. I imagine because she was obese, she wanted to make sure I wouldn't be. But looking back at childhood pictures, I was never really fat as a child. When I was about five years old, you might say I still had some baby fat, but you would never describe me as being fat. If I must say so myself, I was kind of cute. Nevertheless my mother told me I had to diet and, therefore I could not have more than one cookie from the box of assorted cookies placed in front of me at the kitchen table. Sometimes, when my mother wasn't looking, I would sneak another cookie. When I was six or seven years old, I remember stealing money from my mother's handbag to buy chocolate covered halvah from the local grocery. It cost three cents and I could get three of them if I stole a dime. I still feel as if I am sneaking food when I eat something I love. And sometimes I still feel guilty when I let it get the better of me: when I eat too much of something delicious. My present desire to eat what I shouldn't probably stems from those experiences. Although I know I am not really fat, I still often think and feel I am. I have worried about how fat I am since I was a little girl. *And I have been dieting ever since.*

I am a psychotherapist in the private practice of treating adults and adolescents. Since going into the field of psychology, I have spent a lot of time thinking about why people overeat. Why were my mother, her sister and brother obese? Why do people spend millions of dollars on one diet book or program after another to lose weight? Why do the people, who finally lose the weight, regain those pounds, plus more?

There are many conscious and obvious reasons we overeat. Eating is pleasurable. Overeating can provide pleasure when we are not getting enough joy out of life. When things are not going well, a hot fudge sundae may make us feel better. Chinese food or Raisinettes do the trick for me. Many people forget their pain or troubles and feel better while they are eating something delicious. Just think how many children are offered an ice cream cone when they fall down and cry. Many parents do what their parents did. They offer something delicious to soothe the hurt. For most of us, soothing pain with something delicious begins very early in life.

I grew up in one of the thousands of apartment buildings in congested Brooklyn, New York. But one summer, when I was seven, we went to "the country." I felt free wandering gleefully around in the woods. It was wonderful. But my joy soon ended. I tripped and fell in the woods and got pebbles in my knee. I remember it as if it were yesterday, though it was decades ago. I ran to my mother crying hysterically and pointing to my bleeding knee. My mother looked down at my bloody knee and then at me. In an attempt to soothe and calm me, she said if I let her take the pebbles out of my knee she would take me to the candy store and I could have anything I wanted. This was extraordinary. I was, after all, the little girl who couldn't even have more than one cookie. Since I knew I was not going to have a choice about having the pebbles taken out of my knee, I made the deal. Picking out all my favorite candies was fantastic. But eating them with my mother there and approving, was ecstasy. Going to the doctor usually brought the same reward: something delicious to eat. It feels childish to admit, but even today, it is difficult for me to go to the doctor or do something else which is painful without rewarding myself with some candy. The desire to soothe or reward myself with candy is still with me some forty odd years later.

James Coco, the actor, says he was a skinny child until he was nine years old. He points to his tonsillectomy as the beginning of his weight problem. "Without that tonsillectomy, I might never have had a weight problem. Though I was terrified at first of surgery, my parents won me over by describing the ice cream feast to come . . . . Visions of Breyer's hand-dipped ice cream danced in my head as I went under the anesthetic — vanilla, chocolate, strawberry, the three main flavors they made then. My last conscious thought was of chocolate."[1] Mr. Coco acknowledges that of course there were other reasons for his overeating. One, he states, is that to him "Food is love."[2]

Overeating can be fun, especially with others. Think about it. What do most people do when they get together? They eat. They eat brunch. They eat lunch. They eat dinner. They eat après dinner. What do we think of when we get together for Easter, Passover, Christmas, Thanksgiving, etc.? What are we going to eat? For weeks ahead of time we plan what we will cook, prepare or eat for our holiday dinners. It has been that way probably since the beginning of time. We celebrate by eating. Eating is how we share a good time and pleasure with others. It is a way of connecting. It is a pleasure both to the senses and to the emotions.

Recently my son had a slumber party. My husband and I understood perfectly when he gave us the long list of "munchies" to buy for the party. For my son and his friends, the best part of the party was eating all the "junk" food they possibly could. Throwing it at each other was an additional delight.

A man I know feared he might have diabetes. Medically he had reason for his fear. We talked about the possibility this fear was related to his mother and father developing adult onset diabetes. But his biggest fear was not that he might have a serious, possibly life threatening disease. His fear was if he did indeed have diabetes, it would prevent him from having desserts. I found that hard to believe. But he said, "Really, I'm serious. One of the biggest pleasures I have in life is sharing desserts with my wife at the end of dinner. It's a big part of our intimacy and fun."

Now with greater public awareness of health issues, we know overeating, fat, cholesterol and sugar are all bad for us. If you eavesdrop on conversations, you can overhear friends relating stories of how they try to trick themselves out of eating all those wonderful, but, alas, bad foods. I, myself, have shared stories with friends about freezing desserts so that I wouldn't eat them, only to discover, when I weakened, that some frozen cakes are even better than fresh cake! One comedian jokes about avoiding the temptation of fattening foods by throwing them away. However, an hour later she finds herself rummaging through her garbage retrieving the forbidden food, brushing it off and eating it. The audience laughs. The audience connects. Often, when we are not eating, we are joking and talking about food. We identify and we connect through food.

Overeating, like smoking or drinking, helps divert some people from feelings of anxiety. When something is going wrong, the first thing overeaters think about is eating. Eating, or more drastically, bingeing, helps assuage the upsetting feelings for the moment. Like when my mother took the pebbles out of my knee, even though it hurt, the hurt is softened by being nurtured. Eating is something we do to divert our attention away from an emotion, even a positive one, that is so intense it doesn't feel comfortable.

Little is said about eating when there is an intense positive emotion. My desire to write this book raised some doubts. I believed it was such an important book; how was it possible no one has written it before? I did a lot of research, reading many books and journal articles about overeating and eating disorders. But in all my research I did not find any book that suggested what I wished to communicate. When I was in the library the last time and realized no one else had written this kind of book, I became extremely excited that writing this book was becoming a very real possibility. **It would be a dream come true to write a book helping people to understand the powerful underlying wishes and fears that cause us to overeat.** I was so excited I didn't know what to do with myself.

At first what I wanted to do was eat and eat a lot. I was not hungry, but that very excited feeling, which was lasting a long time, began to feel very uncomfortable. Eating would be a way to calm myself a little, (I did not want to lose all of the excitement, but just quiet it a little.) I wanted to mollify the pleasurable and happy, but too intense, feeling of excitement. Ironically, here I was thinking about writing a book about overeating, and precisely at that moment what I was thinking about doing was overeating! Ultimately I told my husband about it, who laughed and shared in the excitement. That, plus beginning to write, was what helped.

Even pleasurable feelings can be uncomfortable. Many people, especially those who do not overeat, would react in the exact opposite way. They would be unable to eat. But overeaters typically rely on food to deal with many things.

For many, one of the most gratifying pleasures in the world is eating. But not all people overeat. It is incomprehensible to someone who overeats, that a person can eat a little of something delicious and not want any more, because he has had enough. When we overeat with a person like that, we feel ashamed of overeating. Intuitively we know there is another reason we are eating too much. Often this shame brings about hiding of, or even self deception about, eating.

My obese mother, used to tell my sister and me that she just could not lose weight. She would tell us how she watched what she ate very carefully, but her body would not comply. Growing up, I felt so badly for her. The shame of her weight affected her whole life. When I was about twelve years old, I found out why she could not lose weight. I was babysitting my younger sister when my mother went out one evening. We both were hungry, so I decided to cook something for us. I went looking in the "pot closets" for the proper pot to make soup. Lo and behold, behind the pots, all kinds of goodies were hidden. There was a large assortment of candy and cake, things my mother never ate openly. Her shame at not being able to resist overeating sweets obviously caused my mother to lie to us and maybe to herself.

Despite these conscious and obvious reasons for overeating, the most compelling reason people overeat is less obvious. Overeating has more to do with unconscious wishes and fears than anything else. Truly! Even though you are certain you want to be thin, if you are consistently overeating, unconscious wishes and fears of being thin most likely exist.

Through my research, study and psychotherapeutic treatment of many people who overeat, as well as supervising other psychotherapists who treat people who overeat, I have developed a good understanding of the psychodynamics of overeating. Volumes have been written about why people overeat and what they can do about it, but little has been written about or even spoken about the unconscious forces that highly influence people's patterns of eating.

When an individual consistently or compulsively overeats, invariably that overeating is unconsciously and symbolically representing something other than just eating. People who overeat may believe their greatest wish is to be thin. But if they are overeating, unconsciously they have other wishes which are even more powerful than their wish to be thin. Overeating may represent an unconscious wish to be fat or a fear of being thin. Upon reading this you may be thinking, "How is that possible? I spend so much time thinking about and wishing I could be thin. Now you're telling me I really want to be fat or I am afraid of being thin?" Yes! If you are consistently overeating that is true. The most important and driving forces underlying overeating are our unconscious wishes and fears. Anyone who consistently overeats does so because of an unconscious wish or fear related to eating or being fat. These wishes and fears are so powerful that the most rigorous dieting is defeated because of them. There is only one way to be healthy and consistently slender: that is to resolve the conscious and unconscious fears or wishes that cause us to overeat.

I'll repeat that last statement because it is so important. THERE IS ONLY ONE WAY TO BE HEALTHY AND CONSISTENTLY SLENDER: THAT IS TO RESOLVE THE CONSCIOUS AND UNCONSCIOUS FEARS OR WISHES THAT CAUSE US TO OVEREAT. Although this statement is probably provocative and disturbing, it is true. This will make more sense as we proceed and gain greater understanding of how our minds work.

Essentially, to successfully lose weight and keep it off, we have to change our diets to include mostly low fat foods and we must exercise. But again *most importantly*, we must resolve the conscious and unconscious wishes we have to be fat.

***

A truly sad story attests to that fact. Michael Hebranko, a forty-three year old man had to have his living room bay window, shrubs and part of an aluminum fence from his front yard removed so that he could be lifted by fork lift and taken to the hospital in a specially constructed ambulance to treat his pneumonia, heart disease, gangrene, fluid in his lungs and collapsed veins. You see, Mr Hebranko weighs about 940 pounds and could not fit through his front door. The tragedy of Mr. Hebranko's story does not end there. Four years ago, Mr. Hebranko was listed in the *Guinness Book of Records* for losing the greatest amount of weight in the shortest period of time. He lost 705 pounds in eighteen months. When asked by reporters why he allowed himself to regain 735 pounds, he was reported as saying, "I took care of the outside problem instead of the inside one."[3]

Two

Fattening Wishes

It is not fun to be overweight. Overweight people are frequently regarded as having emotional problems. In fact, several of my patients have said the greatest shame about their weight is being thought of as emotionally inferior. The overweight are definitely stigmatized. A Long Island newspaper recently reported how a decorated and dedicated fireman for the Wantagh Fire Department was told that because of his weight he would not be sworn in as a second assistant chief, a post to which he was elected.[4] Even though he was a hero and exceptionally qualified, he was told his weight would cause him to forfeit this position.

In the biography *Oprah!*, by Robert Waldron,[5] Oprah Winfrey is quoted about her struggle with overeating. She said when people told her to use will power and just close her mouth, she felt like slapping them. For her and many others, control over eating is very difficult and often even impossible.

Many people think the overweight have no control over themselves. They regard them as weak and lacking in will power. Actually overeaters are not any weaker than anyone else. In addition to possible conscious conflicts, people who are significantly overweight harbor unconscious wishes or fears related to eating. That is the reason they are not in control of their overeating. Of course unconscious wishes and fears can affect virtually all aspects of one's life, but they are not always as apparent as overeating. When we think, even deeply, about why we are fat, we can only be aware of our conscious wishes and fears. Our unconscious wishes and fears are not accessible to us.

Sometimes an unconscious wish may conflict with another unconscious wish. Or an unconscious wish may conflict with a conscious wish. For example we may consciously wish to be loving towards our spouse, however unconsciously we may harbor aggressive wishes. We may consciously wish to have many friends but also have a desire not to risk any social disappointment.

When our wishes are in conflict, our egos find a way to deal with the conflict in the least anxiety provoking way possible. In psychoanalytic terms this resolution is called a "compromise solution." Unconsciously and without awareness, our ego finds a solution to our conflicting wishes, one that causes the least discomfort. This compromise formation often appears as a symptom.

Ironically for the overeater, more often than not, the compromise solution is to be fat. *As outrageous as it may sound, the solution that results in the least amount of anxiety is to overeat and look fat.* Of course this solution is not usually what is consciously experienced. In fact consciously, the person may be feeling a great deal of anxiety about being overweight. If you ask an overweight woman (or man) what his or her wish would be if granted the three proverbial wishes by a fairy godmother, it would not be uncommon for the answer to be an immediate "Of course, to be thin." However, if this person is overeating, a different, unconscious wish is prevailing. Clearly then, overeating is the compromise that brings about the least possible pain or anxiety. That does not mean that overeating eliminates anxiety. It usually does not. What it does mean is, that given all the person's conscious and unconscious wishes, the behavior that results in the least anxiety and discomfort, is overeating. Truly, being thin may result in even greater anxiety for the overeater.

Cara, a thirty-six year old obese woman, noticed her reflection in a store window and was appalled. She felt repulsed by what she saw. She usually avoided mirrors, so this reflection was startling. She thought, "That's it, I'm going on a strict diet." She had a glimmer of her unconscious wish however, when she subsequently thought, "Maybe not. At least I'm safe this way." Her conscious wish was not to look fat. However her unconscious wish, the one that wins out over and over, was "I want to be fat because it keeps me safe." Why being fat allows some people to feel safe, will become clearer as we go on.

The kind of obesity I am addressing is due to overeating. I am not referring to people who, due to their genetic inheritance, energy use or other physiological factors, maintain more body weight than they wish.

Three

Our Unconscious

Unconscious wishes are so powerful they exert tremendous control over all our behavior. The conscious wish of the person who wants to be thin is not to overeat. The unconscious wish of the person who overeats however, is so powerful, that despite the strength of the conscious wish, there is tremendous difficulty controlling overeating. People who overeat know this intuitively. They know there is something else causing their lack of control over eating. However since it is unconscious, they are unaware of what it is. They cannot understand why their eating is out of control. They end up feeling weak, inadequate and ashamed. They should not feel that way, because unless their unconscious wishes or fears are resolved, their eating, to a large extent is out of their control.

Although Sigmund Freud's theories have lost mainstream popularity, he was the first to enlighten us about how our wishes and fears, buried in our unconscious, are the power behind our actions. Although they are beyond our awareness, those wishes influence our behavior in significant ways. I will tell you a modern version of an example Freud used to demonstrate the unconscious.[6]

We can compare the unconscious to a lobby at a fine restaurant called "The Conscious." This restaurant is the "in" place to go. The lobby, named "The Unconscious," is filled with many different people pressing to gain entrance to "The Conscious." Let us say the people waiting represent different impulses such as anger and sexual feelings. Between the lobby, "The Unconscious," and the entrance to the restaurant, "The Conscious," is a bouncer nicknamed "The Censor." His job is to prevent all those people (actually impulses) he deems unacceptable from entering the restaurant. He usually rejects certain aggressive or sexual types that are not wanted in the restaurant. His is a very important job. He wants to keep out all those elements the establishment, "The Conscious," believes are dangerous. With so many in the lobby, "The Unconscious," pressing to get in, "The Censor" has to be vigilant that none of them sneak in. Also, he needs to recognize any who managed to sneak in and get rid of them. He needs to be on his toes to allow entrance to only those which are acceptable to "The Conscious." Most of the time he is successful. Sometimes he is not. When he is not successful, problems result in the place called "The Conscious." In fact, "The Conscious" sometimes suffers from the mere fact that the undesirables in "The Unconscious" exist.

You can readily see that the unconscious is filled with many ideas that we want to keep out of our conscious awareness. We are not aware of the many thoughts, impulses, fantasies and feelings in our unconscious mind. They are kept in our unconscious mind, out of our awareness, because those thoughts seem threatening to our conscious mind.

Charles Brenner, in *An Elementary Textbook of Psychoanalysis*,[7] offers evidence of the unconscious with an example of someone under hypnosis. A man is hypnotized and given an autohypnotic suggestion to open a window when the clock strikes two. While under the trance he is told he will not remember anything that happened during the trance when he awakens. When he wakes up and the clock strikes two, the man goes over and opens up the window. If he is asked why he opened the window, he will respond either "I don't know" or "I just felt like it." More likely he will give a rationalization, like he was warm. Actually he is not conscious of the real reason he opened the window, nor can he become conscious of it by trying to remember. The action, which was induced by the unconscious, is completed without any accurate understanding of why it was done.

***

Unconscious thoughts are also demonstrated by the commonplace slip of the tongue. For example, Bob, a patient I saw for therapy, was very angry with his boss, but unaware of his anger. His boss called a sales meeting at 6 a.m., although his boss was fully aware that Bob lived two hours from work. This meant Bob would have to leave his house at four in the morning to arrive at the meeting on time. Bob told his boss, "I'll be *mad*, I mean glad, to come to the six a.m. sales meeting." His embarrassment, correcting the slip, revealed that on some level he knew his real feeling had slipped out. He insisted, however, he was not aware of his resentment towards his boss, until his slip of the tongue occurred. Bob is an ambitious, hardworking and conscientious man. He likes to think of himself as someone who is responsible and accepts doing whatever needs to be done. It is unacceptable for him to think he would resent any job he is asked to do. The feelings about his insensitive boss and how angry he was at him were repressed, only to be revealed by his slip of the tongue.

***

Freud himself confided that his unconscious motives were being expressed in his own behavior when he visited patients. He noticed he only forgot to visit nonpaying patients. With this anecdote, he pointed out that although he agreed to see patients free of charge, he had repressed what was in his unconscious: that he resented doing so. His generosity was belied by his forgetfulness.[8]

***

Forgetting is a very common illustration of unconscious wishes being enacted. My husband is a forgetter. He is such a good, kind, man, he has a difficult time saying no to anyone, even though his work load is overwhelming. So he forgets. Actually he would be better off saying no, because his forgetting often causes someone (especially me) to be angry with him, instead of just feeling disappointed. By forgetting, his unconscious thought or wish is being acted out; he does not want to do what he said he would. This type of forgetting is often related to anger. In a passive way he is expressing the anger about being overburdened which he cannot express verbally.

***

The expression of unconscious wishes are experienced by everyone. Years ago I was driving on the Long Island Expressway to meet a friend at her home on Long Island, when a very confusing event took place. Instead of getting off at my friend's exit, I ended up at the Midtown Tunnel heading toward Manhattan, about 20 minutes past her exit. I just could not believe it! I had to pay the toll, go through the tunnel, find a street to turn around, pay another toll, get back into the tunnel heading east, and drive back on the Long Island Expressway to my friend's exit. With all the extra driving, I had plenty of time to think about why I had driven all the way into New York City. The motivation for my drive to the city was completely outside my consciousness, but I ultimately realized what it was about. I was driving towards the home of a man with whom I had been in a love relationship. It ended six months before and I had believed I was better off. Obviously what was buried in my unconscious was that I missed him and wished to be with him again. Most of us have had the experience of passing the place of our destination. Upon reflection, we can sometimes recognize either we did not actually want to go there or preferred to be elsewhere.

***

Dreams are another reflection of unconscious thoughts. Unacceptable thoughts, wishes and fears, which are repressed and unconscious, can be symbolically expressed in disguised form in a dream.

A female patient was sabotaging her success in her own psychotherapy career because she feared I would be angry with her for competing with me. She dreamed she was going on stage for her acting debut. She glanced into the audience and saw a famous actress she admired. Feeling frightened this actress would be angry with her if she played the part for which this actress was famous, she decided to step down from the stage and let the famous actress do the part. In this dream she abandons her desired goals fearing that I, symbolized by the famous actress in the dream, would be angry with her if she became a star in my field.

***

Our unconscious wishes and fears, even though we are unaware of them, are often more powerful than our conscious thoughts. Because we have no awareness of them, we have no control over them. Unconscious wishes are the power behind much of what we do. They can significantly affect our choice of work, of a mate, of the ability or not to finish things, our sexual desires, various physical disorders, whether or not we succeed, whether we are dare devils or introverts, what colors we choose, what kind of clothes we wear, whether or not we marry, whether or not we want children, our ability to protect ourselves, our desire or ability to relate to people, the way we relate to spouses, children, bosses or friends and much, much more.

***

Unconscious wishes and fears significantly influence overeating. Bulimia and Anorexia Nervosa are eating disorders based on unconscious, as well as conscious conflicts, wishes and fears. Consistent overeating is also based on unconscious as well as conscious conflicts, wishes and fears.

Four

Wishes Can Come True

What can we do to lose weight when contradictory wishes may be harbored in our unconscious? And if these wishes are unconscious, how can we even know what they are?

We can begin by surmising that if a medical or metabolical problem does not exist and we are consistently unable to lose weight or keep it off, that some other force is operating. We may only be aware of the wish to be thin, however if we continue to overeat we must recognize that another wish does exist, be it conscious or unconscious. Our wish to be thin must be the *predominant* wish over all our other wishes for it to be fulfilled. If losing weight and being thin is our predominant wish, overriding not only our wish to eat all the delicious things we desire, but also our unconscious wishes, then we WILL LOSE WEIGHT and be as thin as our body shape will allow us to be. Since as adults we and we alone are in control of our body, if we resolve other wishes which run counter to our wish to be thin, WE WILL BE THIN. But to do so, it must be the predominant wish. *All* wishes must be superseded by our one conscious wish to be thin.

When our conscious wish to be thin predominates, we will be compelled to follow a diet and exercise regime which will result in our bodies looking the way we wish. We may discover that we have two contradictory conscious wishes. For example, we may realize that we wish to have a body like a supermodel but also wish to enjoy gourmet dining. These wishes are probably contradictory. Most supermodels maintain their weight by eating lots of low calorie salads and following a daily rigorous exercise program. You may realize that you wish to be thin, but not at the price of giving up eating what you like. To be successful you will have to give up one wish or moderate both wishes. You can possibly accept being a size 10 or 12 dress instead of a size 6 and eat more of what you like. Or you may decide being a size 6 is worth giving up the food you love, and develop a love for delicious salads. Of course we cannot be successful if we wish to be size 6 and wish to eat all and everything we want. But we may be able to, with a good exercise regime, eat a little of everything we like.

***

If recognizing and accepting this you still wish to lose weight and be thin, the next step is to become aware of what contrary wishes exist in other levels of your mind. You must identify your wishes to continue to overeat or to remain fat and either resolve them or make them less powerful.

To become aware of what contrary wishes exist that prevent you from fulfilling your conscious wish to lose weight, will take some work. If you think you do not really want to be bothered working hard for this knowledge or you do not really have the time or patience to do that, what do you think that means? Of course! It is an obvious sign your wish to lose weight is not your most powerful wish. At least it is not greater than your wish not to have to expend too much effort to do so. If you did have a thought such as that, do not despair. Actually, that kind of thought can function as blatant proof of the existence of your contrary wishes. Those contrary wishes may merely reflect not wishing to exert any effort or not having the time to discover what other obstacles exist. But most likely, those reasons are just covering up your more powerful unconscious wishes to stay overweight.

***

Once you have decided that losing weight is <u>so</u> important you are willing to devote much time and energy to it, you can begin to do what is necessary to lose the weight you wish to. The first step is to become aware of what unconscious wishes may exist to bring about *your wish to be fat or fear of being thin!* As you read this book and become aware of the many issues that bring about wishes to be fat or fears of being thin, you may find yourself feeling defensive, scornful or rejecting outright what you are reading about. Recognize these responses as possible further signs of the wishes and fears that exist within you which are promoting your wanting to remain fat. Remember, the only way to succeed in being slim is for your conscious wish to be predominant over all other wishes. Therefore, if something you read seems preposterous, irrelevant or boring, before devaluing it consider the possibility that a nerve has been touched and continue to read on and consider seriously what is being said.

Reread those cases which make you feel uncomfortable and ask yourself what about them makes you uncomfortable. Do you identify with this person's story? Are your family dynamics similar? Do you behave in similar ways? Does this person's feelings and thoughts echo your own?

We have all gone through each developmental stage of childhood and so it would not be surprising if you identify with several of the case studies presented. It is essential for us to understand that there is not a thought, feeling, or wish that is bad. We all have aggressive, possessive, envious, sexual and hostile feelings and thoughts, whether or not we are aware of them. To witness little children playing is to see the expression of a complete range of human feelings. Having a thought, be it angry or envious, is not equal to acting out that thought and hurting someone.

To begin to discover your harbored wishes that exist contrary to your conscious wish to be thin, I suggest that you reread the cases in this book with which you felt identified, which felt familiar, and those which made you feel uncomfortable. Thoughts, feelings and wishes which are unconscious, are unconscious for a reason; if they were conscious they would cause us discomfort. Therefore we can assume that something that makes a connection to our unconscious thoughts, may result in our feeling somewhat uncomfortable.

If you are having trouble thinking about a particular case or issue that is discussed because it is too uncomfortable, put the book down for a day or two and then go back to it. The discomfort is pointing to something about this case that is significant for you. When you return to that case, see if you can stay with it long enough to identify what it is about that case that is disturbing to you.

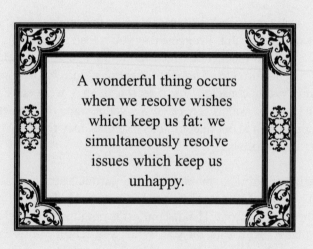

A wonderful thing occurs when we resolve wishes which keep us fat: we simultaneously resolve issues which keep us unhappy.

Part Two

Hungry for You

At times it is truly
astonishing to discover
wishes, of which before,
we were unaware.

One

Hungry for You

```
                    Mother
            Me          You
      Together      As          One
As              I           Need          You
                    Mother
```

— Diane Fero

Some people who maintain a wish for an intimate connection or merger with their mother, may do so unconsciously, through their first association to mother: that is *eating*. Since from infancy on, nourishment and nurturance are associated with mother, some people *unconsciously overeat as a way of symbolically recovering the feeling of the lost union with their mother. Eating, for them, is not to assuage real hunger, but hunger for the feeling of oneness with their mother.*

From the beginning of our lives, eating and therefore the feeling of being taken care of and loved, is profoundly connected to our mothers. As newborn infants our pleasure is related to two things: the feeling of comfort or oneness in our mother's arms and the sucking and drinking milk from or near her breast. (I will use mother throughout this book when referring to the person who maintains the caretaker functions for the child.) In a satisfactory mother-infant relationship, the most important part of our mother's relationship to us is our care and feeding. As infants, our earliest experience is of our mother rescuing us from hunger and pain. Also, hopefully, of her smiling, talking, singing and joyfully responding to us as she is feeding us. As infants, we experience our mother as one with us. It seems to us, as if she is aware of our every need and that she is happy to take care of it. When she provides us with nourishment, milk, our hunger is assuaged. When she holds us in her arms and enjoys our cooing, we feel both safety and pleasure. From the time of earliest infancy, eating, physical nourishment and nurturance are inseparable from our mothers. The earliest and most significant relationship we have is with our mother taking care of us and feeding us.

Symbiosis refers to this phase of our infancy in which our mother, when she is attuned to us, feels a need and desire to respond to and take care of all of our needs. Our mother's and our needs dovetail. It is as pleasurable for our mother, in satisfactory situations, to cradle and feed us, as it is for us to be cradled and fed. Anyone who has witnessed a mother cradling her baby during and after a feeding can see, reflected on both mother and baby's faces, the look of contentment. During our very first stage of being we, as infants, experience ourselves merged and one with our mothers.

When we suck at our mother's breast we experience a sense of well being and satisfaction. This feeling is what we refer to when we speak of "childhood bliss." Certainly we cannot remember that time in our lives, but we can undoubtedly imagine how wonderful it was to have our every need happily satisfied by someone who loved us. That time in our lives was so gratifying, many people actively attempt to reexperience it in their adult relationships. Some people seek a mate who will perfectly respond to their every need: a partner whose sole interest is to fulfill their desires. If their partner has his or her own needs it feels to them like an abandonment. The search for a partner who is perfectly in tune with his or her lover's wish, harks back to that wonderful blissful time of mother-infant union.

To find a mate whose needs merge with ours however, is totally impossible; for no adult can have all his needs met by another. It is too bad, because it seems as if it would be wonderful. Actually, it has its shortcomings. You cannot be an independent person while still merged with another. Those who seek a mate who will satisfy all his or her needs feel consistently frustrated and let down. The fact that the state of oneness can never exist again, as it did in infancy, brings about many failed relationships and much pain and disappointment. Often the disappointment is attributed to a lack in the other person. Rather, it should be seen for what it is: the striving for an impossible dream, an experience that can only be fulfilled in infancy.

The longing to regain this feeling of oneness is universal. Actually the longing for oneness can be fulfilled, but just for moments at a time. For example, in moments during sex we can achieve that wonderful experience of oneness, of shared boundaries and shared pleasure. Some people experience that feeling of oneness with nature, some with art, some with music. When we achieve it, it does feel wonderful. However, to ultimately be the person who we are or who we want to be, a person with autonomy and individuality, we must give up that blissful state of symbiosis. We must give it up in order to grow.

When a symbiotic, that is, a reciprocally merged relationship between mother and child, continues beyond infancy, it becomes a pathological state. Psychotherapists refer to that kind of a relationship as "parent and child enmeshment." It is a relationship whereby neither parent nor child can allow the other to live an independent life.

Alice

Alice, a thirty-four year old woman I worked with in psychoanalysis, had a mother who insisted on continuing a symbiotic-like relationship with her daughter. Her mother would emphatically withdraw and emotionally abandon Alice, refusing to talk to her for days at a time, whenever she, as a child, showed any indication of being different or separate from her mother. If Alice's mother liked subdued colors and Alice showed enthusiasm for bright colors, Alice's mother would emotionally withdraw, after indicating to Alice that bright colors were a rejection of her own good taste. Consequently, Alice began to appreciate subdued colors. When Alice chose to be with friends after school rather than with her mother, her mother would sulk and tell Alice she should not worry about leaving her old mother lonely. Soon after, Alice preferred her mother's company. Anything Alice did which reflected her own individuality, such as liking rock bands, was received by her mother as a threat or rejection.

This relationship continued into Alice's adulthood. Alice responded to her mother's messages by doing what she wanted to and subsequently feeling guilty or more often, responding to her mother's needs. Gradually and subtly Alice became more and more like her mother. This brought about loving and enthusiastic responses from her mother. Alice's mother was obese, and Alice became obese. Her obesity demonstrated oneness with her mother and therefore assured her mother's love. Her obesity and overeating also symbolically recreated for her the merged feeling of mother and child for which Alice still yearned.

Two

Loss of Childhood Bliss

Hilde Bruch, an expert on eating disorders, found that mothers of obese children often interfere with their child separating. She said these mothers are overprotective and induce dependency in their children. They offer an overabundance of food to their children, not for nutritional purposes, but as a substitute for other needs of the child or for the mother's own dependency needs. This excessive and inappropriate feeding contributes to the child's ultimate inability to distinguish between hunger, satiation, and other feelings.[9]

We know from the research done by Margaret Mahler,[10] a certain predictable development unfolds for each of us who are fortunate enough to have a healthy childhood. When we, as infants, have had sufficient and secure satisfaction of our physical and emotional needs, we begin a process of separating and individuating, that is differentiating ourselves from our mother. This is brought about by our increasing abilities to move around and communicate. Our interests in the outside world begin to develop. When we are about ten to fifteen months old, we enter, what is referred to as, the "practicing stage." At this stage we, as toddlers, virtually have a "love affair with the world."[11] At the beginning of this stage, as long as our mother is within sight or sound, we go on wonderful adventures expanding our world. Now, we are more interested in the outside world than in our mother. However our confidence exists only as long as we can see or hear our mother. In fact, when our mother leaves the room, we, as toddlers, become temporarily upset with her when she returns: angry at her for abandoning us.

Months later in our development, we act as if we are completely oblivious to our mother's existence. We feel all powerful and seem to believe we can do anything we wish to with impunity. We get great pleasure testing out our abilities to move around, explore and master the world around us. We feel full of ourselves and on top of the world. Seeing us prance around gives the observer the impression we certainly think we are the greatest.

When we move out of the symbiotic phase we still have, for a while, the illusion of a dual unity with our mother. We still believe that we and mother are somehow one, and that we share what appears to be mother's omnipotence. After all, she knows when we need to eat, when we need to sleep, how to fix our boo boos. However, by the sixteenth month, we become increasingly aware of our physical separateness; for instance, when we fall down and hurt ourselves and our mother is not automatically there. This event brings about a great deal of anxiety for us. Our cognitive development has brought about the realization that we are helpless by ourselves and completely dependent on our mother. We become aware that our mother is not part of us. Our illusion of omnipotence is shattered. No longer are we oblivious to our need for our mother.

Because of this state of affairs, we feel a resurgence of dependency feelings toward our mother. We insist mother share every activity with us in order to make sure she is continually present. When we succeed in getting our mother's attention, our anxiety about our separateness from her is temporarily assuaged. During this phase, we attempt to coerce our mother to be with us at every moment. Only in this way, can we reestablish our wish that we are merged and one with mother. However, we find out this is not possible. Our mother will just not cooperate. She refuses to continually be with us. Therefore, we are forced to recognize our mother's separateness from us. This is a painful time, a time of crisis for all of us, as toddlers. It is a time of mood swings. Due to the resumption of our dependency feelings on our mother, this subphase is called "rapproachment."

The phase of rapprochement often brings about difficulties and misunderstandings between us and our mothers. From our mother's point of view, we are not as physically dependent as we were six months ago, so why are we now more insistent on her undivided attention? It seems that one minute we want to get away from her control and the next we refuse to leave her side.

Whether we succeed in separating from our mother and achieving a sense of independence from her is significantly influenced by the way she responds to our efforts. Those of us who do best during this phase are the ones whose mother can accept our resurgence of dependency needs and respond to them in stride.

However, some mothers cannot accept the child's renewed dependence and demandingness. These mothers may respond to their clinging toddlers by pushing them away and rejecting them. Unfortunately, this reaction often results in more clinging on the toddler's behalf and then more rejection.

Some mothers welcome or even encourage their toddler becoming more dependent again. These mothers desire very close contact between themselves and their child and are distressed when their child is becoming more independent. Instead of feeling delighted about their child's growing up, they experience it as a loss, a loss of their "baby." Some mothers plan to become pregnant at this time, so they can reexperience that feeling of co-dependence with a newborn.

Parents who want their child to be dependent and compliant, convey these feelings to their child through both verbal and non-verbal behaviors. This often undermines the child's own normal desire to separate and move away from his or her mother. When the mother responds unenthusiastically to these normal desires, the child often will be less adventuresome and less likely to individuate. The child learns that staying close to mother brings back her enthusiasm towards him.

Three

Eating to Recover the Lost Union

*E*ating, with its accompanying blissful feeling of being nurtured and *fed, is a way many people with difficulties separating from their mothers, unconsciously attempt to bring about a feeling of reunion.* Unconsciously, eating and being nourished echos feelings experienced when we were one with our mothers. M. Sperling,[12] an expert on eating disorders, indicates that eating symbolizes merger with the other. This symbolic merger, she states, is used by overeaters to prevent the feeling of aloneness. Sperling described food as the semisymbolic equivalent of the mother.

Anna Freud stated that by the age of two, food and mother become consciously separated. However, she said, in the unconscious the connection between the two remains intact.[13] Early feeding experiences and the associated feelings of emotional and physical nurturance, are internalized by us as infants. They are taken into our minds through memory traces of our experiences. And even though we no longer remember them, they stay within our unconscious forever.

Analyzing the dreams of food and eating of his patients, Walter W. Hamburger, M.D.,[14] concluded that the typical eating dream may be translated in the following way: "My infantile longings to be cared for by my loving mother are no longer possible. Instead, I must gratify myself with the recollection of the food which (symbolically) signifies my mother's love."

Separation from our mother, the feeling of being a separate, distinct individual from our mother, is a developmental achievement that should take place in our early childhood. Individuation, becoming an individual different from our mother, is another developmental achievement that should take place in our early childhood. However, separation and individuation are quite difficult feats for many people. The recognition of separateness from mother causes many individuals serious problems. It brings about a feeling of being all alone, unloved and unprotected. For example, Rachel, a forty year old legal secretary, says the reason she cannot leave her mother's home is because there would be no one to take care of her if she, herself, got sick. She is unable to experience herself as competent to take care of herself and her own needs. Feeling competent, for Rachel, is equated with aloneness.

People who have problems separating use methods that evoke the least possible anxiety to deal with these difficulties. Some people literally stay close to their mother and behave very much like their mother or the way their mother wants them to behave. Some people eat as a way to symbolically reconnect with their mother of early childhood.

Four

Merged or Lonely

Only if we can experience a satisfactory resolution of the separation-individuation phase of our childhood can we achieve a stable sense of ourselves and others. Our sense of inner security is also dependent on this achievement. But the process of separation is fraught with difficulty. Recognizing that we are not merged with our mother, do not share one boundary with her and therefore are not all-powerful, is traumatic for each of us. Becoming aware that our mother is not concerned exclusively with our needs and welfare is also traumatic.

Whether this trauma will have a lasting deleterious effect on us or not, will depend on how gradually we recognize our state of separateness from our mother. If our recognition of our separateness is allowed to develop gradually and there are enough positive feelings from our mother to reassure and assist us in separating, the trauma of separation should not cause us permanent difficulties. If, on the other hand, awareness of our separateness is more sudden, due to loss of our mother, emotionally or physically, or if our mother is reluctant to allow us to separate, we may assume there will be ongoing difficulties.

Even when the separation process has the support of a "good enough" mother, separating from our mother is a crisis for every one of us. We experience a great deal of conflict during the rapprochement period, that stage in our early childhood when we recognize our separateness from, and our dependency on, our mother. On one hand, we want to gain our own autonomy, independence, assertion and control. But on the other hand, we still yearn for closeness and merger with our mother. This stage of our life causes us to have intense feelings of ambivalence, both wanting our mother at our side and not wanting her so close. It is a time of ambitendency, of wanting to walk away from our mothers and be independent and wanting to be very close to her and merge. No distance from mother feels comfortable. Closeness feels safe but arouses the dread of fusion. Being apart enhances our feeling of mastery but evokes feelings of loneliness.

Many psychopathological difficulties derive from this phase of development. Several psychoanalysts connect agoraphobia and claustrophobia to the issue of how far or how close to get to the mother of childhood. Margaret Mahler[15] refers to man's eternal struggle between the longing to merge and the fear of engulfment and between the fear of fusion and the fear of isolation. Many analysts write about how this period of a child's life and how the struggle between too much closeness or too much distance affects psychopathology. The conflict regarding how close or distant to be from another recurs in later stages of life, such as adolescence and marriage, and is never fully resolved.

Five

"The Pounds Have Been Melting Away"

Many people who have problems separating, assuage those painful feelings of separateness and longing for mother, through regressive fantasies. These unconscious fantasies symbolically recreate the blissful feeling of oneness and the feeling of being nurtured and loved. This kind of fantasy is often connected to overeating. Eating, as we know, is the earliest connection to the all giving mother of early childhood. For some people eating, unconsciously, evokes the fantasy of being one with mother again. The feeling of pain over separateness is forgotten through food.

Recognizing the significance of the wish for merger with mother in schizophrenics, some psychoanalysts constructed a study to see if a subliminal message, "mommy and I are one,"[16] administered to schizophrenic patients, would result in a decrease of their symptoms. The study was devised to arouse symbiotic-like fantasies. In the study, schizophrenic men looked into a tachistoscope and received a subliminal message that said, "mommy and I are one." A control group was exposed to other messages. As hypothesized, the exposure to the message, "mommy and I are one," did indeed reduce symptoms in the schizophrenic patients.

Later, the investigators decided to study whether the exposure to the subliminal message, "mommy and I are one," could help obese women lose weight. The study consisted of two groups. One group received the subliminal message, "mommy and I are one." The control group was given the subliminal message, "people are walking." The study involved thirty overweight women who were given weekly counseling sessions dealing with how to control their weight. The study went on for twelve weeks. Each week in addition to their counseling session, the women looked into a tachistoscope and were exposed to one of the subliminal messages.

The results were fascinating. One woman who requested to be part of this study lost twenty pounds in two months. However this particular woman was in the control group and was told that she was at the beginning of the study. Other individuals, who received the oneness stimulus, also lost this amount of weight in the same time period. But no other woman in the control group lost near this amount of weight. The researchers were perplexed. The woman, when asked about this strange occurrence explained that initially when she discovered she was only permitted to be in the control group, she was disappointed. However, the researchers had described the study to her and the subliminal message to which the other group would be exposed. She then realized that she could do the same with self hypnosis, something she learned in the past. So every night she put herself in a light trance and repeated over and over again, "mommy and I are one, mommy and I are one." She said, "The pounds have been melting away."[17]

Ann

Ann, a lawyer, was a thirty-six year old, attractive, divorced woman when I began to see her. She was always very attached to her mother. Both she and her mother loved their attachment. They believed they had the ideal relationship. As an adolescent, Ann remembers being different from her friends. All the other teenagers talked about their parents in negative ways and sought to get away from home as often as possible. But Ann preferred staying home or going shopping with her mother. Her mother always told her, "I am your best friend and your only real friend." Ann agreed. In fact, Ann felt she was luckier than all of her friends. While they argued with their mothers and acted rebelliously, Ann felt completely fulfilled in her mother's company. They were so close that any one else around was usually considered an intruder. Ann's mother even discouraged her from having much of a relationship with her father. Ann grew up thinking she wanted to be just like her mother.

Ann indeed was very much like her mother. She recalled that when she married, she selected a man whom her mother liked. In her marriage she would fight with her husband in exactly the same way her mother fought with her father. Ann wanted so much to be like her mother, when she was in the supermarket she would think before choosing an item, "Would my mother get this brand?" She and her mother bought clothing for each other. Doing so was easy, because they wore exactly the same style and size of clothes. She was happy to be and do exactly what her mother would have done. This made her feel very secure and loved.

Most of her life Ann was not really overweight. At times she might have been ten to fifteen pounds over what she would have desired. However, when she believed she was getting too fat, she, usually accompanied by her mother, went on a diet and took the weight off.

When her marriage failed, however, everything changed. She became angry at her mother, blaming her mother for the breakup of her marriage. Her mother, actually did not have anything to do with her marital breakup, but because Ann depended completely on her and still believed she knew best, Anne thought that somehow, her failed marriage was her mother's fault. Her mother, she thought, should have brought her up better or taught her the right way to hold onto a man. Before, there was no question that everything her mother did was perfect. Now Ann questioned everything her mother ever did and said. She questioned why her mother treated her father the way she did, why she refused to respect him. She questioned why she would never travel or go on vacation with her father. She questioned her mother's insistence on only certain brands of food and clothing. Everything she had accepted as truth was now being challenged.

Ann began to pick fights with her mother, opposing her at every opportunity. She devalued how her mother and, therefore she, dressed, perceiving her clothes to be staid and old fashioned. She dramatically changed how she dressed. She disapproved of the tone of voice her mother used with people, and recognizing that she used the same tone of voice upset her. The critical, angry questioning and challenging of her mother was intense and unremitting. Now she was striving to be completely unlike her mother. She began to remember terrible and rejecting things her mother did to her as a child, things she had previously repressed. These memories intensified her anger and challenges to her mother, and her determination to be nothing like her.

But the angrier she became with her mother, the more she ate. The more she raged about how she wanted to be nothing like her mother, the more she ate. The more she became different from her mother, the more she ate.

What was happening to Ann was she had never really emotionally separated or individuated from her mother. Unconsciously, she continued to feel she could not survive without her mother being in charge and taking care of her. Eating, for Ann, expressed her unconscious wish to continue to be attached to her mother and not separate from her. Actually, Ann was still hungry for and unable to let go of her mother. Only by developing an awareness of her unconscious wishes, was Ann able to begin to resolve her feelings about her mother and truly individuate, that is, become a distinct and unique individual.

Six

Nuturing Ourselves Emotionally

Throughout this book we will discuss several unconscious wishes connected with the desire to overeat or stay overweight. The desire to feel one with the nurturing mother, or be close to her or undo the loss of her, reflect one wishful theme. What can we do when we become aware that our reason for overeating is to fulfill this need?

I shared with you a study that was done exposing obese women to the subliminal message "mommy and I are one." The women receiving this message did lose weight. What this tells us is that when some form of mother was obtained, (symbolically and subliminally) the women no longer had to take her in symbolically through food. One woman in the control group who did not hear the subliminal message, lost the same amount of weight, 20 pounds, as the women who did hear the message. When asked to explain, she stated that she discovered the message the other women were receiving and decided to give it to herself. She put herself in a light trance and repeated over and over again, "mommy and I are one."

You can try this yourself. Put yourself in a state of deep relaxation. To do this lie or sit in a comfortable position. Make sure your head is supported. Take a deep breath, then let it out. Do that three times and then breathe normally. Focus your thoughts on your head. Tense your head as tightly as you possibly can, then let it go as limp as you can. Tense your head again, then let it go. Next do the same with your eyes, your mouth, your cheeks, your ears and your neck. Go down your entire body and do the same with each individual part of your body. Take your time doing this. When you have finished you should be completely limp and relaxed. Now think the words "mommy and I are one." Think this thought over and over again for 5 minutes. You can do this exercise once or twice daily.

Another way to do this exercise is to pretape the message "mommy and I are one" and listen to it while in a state of deep relaxation. Make sure to say the words slowly and in a calming manner. If you wish, you can use the tape I have prepared with different exercises on it.

***

Another method to eliminate overeating which is connected to longing for closeness or merger with a nurturing mother, is the following: Before you actually act on your desire to eat what you know will divert you from your goal of losing weight, commit yourself to stop and delay eating for just 10 minutes. Remind yourself that you want to be slim. Recognize *you* are in charge of your body and can eat whatever you want, but you definitely want to be thin. Let yourself know what your eating is really about. Help yourself recognize the feeling of being nurtured when eating will be short lived. Think about all the people who do care about you and can offer you real nurturance and caring. It may be helpful to talk to one of them now and allow yourself to feel nurtured in that way. That is the rationale of the successful program of Overeaters Anonymous. Find other ways to nurture yourself. Think about what good things have happened to you lately. Develop a plan to put more real loving and nurturance into your life. Promise to buy yourself something special that will make you feel good. Distract yourself by going for a walk or in some other way and acknowledge and feel proud you were able to do so. Whip up a delicious diet substitute. Give yourself a hug, or ask a friend for one. Get a massage. Have a cry if you need to.

***

If you are successful and felt nurtured without turning to the fattening food, praise and reward yourself. You did a great job. Recognize this achievement and the knowledge that you can nurture yourself.

***

If you were successful not eating the fattening food for ten minutes but afterwards could not quiet the need to do so, then do so. However be aware of why you are eating what you are. Allow yourself to know that you did well postponing your eating for ten minutes and helping yourself to understand why you were eating. Think about what you can add to your life that will substitute for food when you have that same yearning for nurturance in the future. Make sure to incorporate those nurturing things into your life. Remember, not doing so means your unconscious wish to be symbolically merged with your mother through overeating, is superceding your wish to be thin. Be determined, and mean it, that the next time you will be more successful substituting a non-fattening form of nurturance for your yearning to feel fed and loved.

***

Many of us feel guilty or ashamed and chastise ourselves when we do not follow our diet exactly. Doing this is destructive and interferes with success. Be kind and loving to yourself. Everyone makes mistakes, veers off the track. Eating something you did not want, means just that. It does not mean you are weak or bad. If you can be more understanding and reassuring towards yourself you will be more likely to succeed. If you had a piece of pie do not think, "Now my diet is over, I'll start tomorrow or Monday." Continue dieting after eating the pie. Your diet does not have to be over; you merely added some calories this day. Perhaps you will compensate for those calories by eating less later or tomorrow. Maybe you will exercise those calories off. In fact you should include some extra calories in your weekly diet to satisfy urges for something sweet or special. To create a diet that is completely unsatisfying will result in failure. The idea is not to see how much deprivation you can tolerate, but to develop a way of eating that will be satisfying and allow you to look the way you wish. The goal is to change the way you eat forever.

Seven

Feast or Famine

Some people, with the aim of protecting themselves from "starving," eat even when they are not hungry. People who do this are ensuring themselves symbolically, that they will be able to survive during situations where there may not be sufficient nurturance, *emotionally or otherwise.*

The fear of starvation is often related to the fear of or actual loss of one's mother. Children are completely dependent on their mothers for eating and survival. A child who recognizes he is not one with or in control of his mother, believes he can starve if his mother does not wish to feed him. Unfortunately, as we know from the media, occasionally this actually does occur. Some mothers actually do not feed their child and the child literally starves to death. Some people, who suffered from inconsistent nurturing as a child, overeat as adults to fend off, at least temporarily, the fear that they will be unfed, alone, forgotten and die.

I see the manifestations of this fear with people who obsessively plan their meals, to make sure they will not "starve." If they are going to be some place without food for too long a period of time, they make sure to eat. We can speculate that these people, as young children, did not experience a sense of certainty or consistency about their needs for physical or emotional nurturance being met.

When a feeling of uncertainty about being nurtured prevails, overeating or bingeing can function as a way to reassure ourselves we have all the nurturance we need.

Lana

Lana, an obese woman I treated, was one of the neglected and abused children we read about in the newspapers. She was abandoned by her mother when she was eight years old. Living in the street, she would dig into garbage cans for crumbs of food in order to eat. At other times she would steal food, or trade sexual favors for food. She was finally rescued, when she was twelve years old, by a group of nuns and brought to an orphanage. When I initially saw her, and for many years thereafter, she was eating as much as she could at a time. She would always buy two of everything. "One to eat and one to save in case I'm hungry, so I'll never starve."

At the beginning of treatment, Lana, although in her forties, was like a very young, unsocialized child. The results of psychological tests administered in the various institutions in which she resided as a child, described her as animalistic. In fact, she would crawl on her hands and knees, make grunting sounds, eat with her hands and use the backyard as a bathroom. During one of our first sessions she told me she wanted to be an elephant. But because she was so frightened and untrusting of me, she would not tell me why for many months. As she began to trust me, she would make drawings of elephants for me. She made many of these drawings for me and one day asked me to hang them up. If I did this, she said, she could pretend I was her mother and I was hanging her drawings on my refrigerator, as she saw another little girl's mother do once. This girl/woman Lana, as a child, would hang out at supermarkets and walk next to women who were leaving the supermarket. She would pretend these women were her mother and hoped other people who looked at them would believe that was true. Eventually, Lana told me why she wanted to be an elephant. She remembered a long time ago that she was told, "Elephants never leave their children."

This poignant story reflects how the need for a dependable mother is of primary importance. The feeling of having a dependable mother protects a child from the fear he or she will starve or be hurt in any way.

Eight

The Ba-Ba

All parents can attest to the fact that soon after their baby was born, he was trying to put his hands in his mouth. Several months later one important toy or object might be substituted on occasion for his hands. Selecting this very special object, a Teddy Bear or a doll or a blanket, is an important step in the process of a child's development. It is the first not-me possession the child makes important. This not-me possession has great significance. It is not just another toy or blanket. It has special magical power.

Mothers and fathers know this through experience. Usually the experience goes something like this. The family gets ready to go out for the day. They are in the car traveling to their destination, perhaps a birthday party, for which they are already late. They are late for an understandable reason. Before they left they had to make sure to take the car seat, the high chair, the play pen, the baby's bottles, the baby's food, the diapers, the baby's medicine, the birthday girl's present, and oh yes, their other child. However, they do not get very far before the baby is crying hysterically. "What's the matter?" they ask. Their one year old says "ba, ba." "Oh my God," screams the mother to the father, "I thought you took ba ba." He says with great irritation, "No, I thought you took it." Well, all parents know the end of this story. The car is turned around, and although they will be late for the birthday party, they cannot continue the trip without going back and getting "ba ba." If they did not, their child would be inconsolable the entire day.

For those readers who are not parents and do not know what a "ba ba" is, a "ba ba" is the exceptional object that the baby has chosen to be his special magical possession. The baby may name it "ba ba" or "ru ru" or whatever the baby is capable of saying when he names it. Once the baby names it, the parents acknowledge its new name and refer to it as such.

My son has a "blank." It was once a "ba." As he developed language it became a "blank." Usually on the weekend he is seen with it wrapped around himself. Actually my son's attachment to his blank is not typical. Children usually give up their ba ba, ru ru or blank, by the time they go to school. The need for it usually fades away and is retired as a memento of things past.

So what makes my son's blank and someone else's daughter's ru ru so special and magical? Commonly, simultaneously with thumb-sucking with one hand, the baby takes an external object, for example, a blanket and puts it in his mouth. The preferred object is usually something soft, and something which has been used in the baby's care. Its softness relates to his mother's softness and the softness of the pillows and blankets he cuddles when mother is not there. It could be a blanket, as with my son, or it could be a soft fluffy Teddy Bear or perhaps a stuffed doll. But there is usually only one chosen object that has the magical qualities, and nothing else will do. No substitutes allowed! This prized possession, after awhile, is usually dirty, and smelly, and in some way or another, falling apart. This preferred object was referred to by D.W. Winnicott[18] as a "transitional object."

This Teddy Bear or "blank" assumes attributes of omnipotence because the baby endows it with magical powers of soothing. It is affectionately cuddled as well as mutilated. It is sucked on and dragged, stamped on and laid upon. Although the transitional object is the first not-me object, it is never completely not-me. That is, it represents mother and her care taking of the baby as well as the baby.

The transitional object functions as a bridge between mother and child, between closeness with mother and separation from her. The baby endows it with the ability to soothe him, to do what mother would normally do when she was there. It calms the baby, the way mother would calm him when he was distressed and it makes the baby feel secure the way mother did. The baby transforms the transitional object into an object which can magically provide comfort. That is why it helps the baby fall asleep or be separate from his mother in general. The transitional object reflects a baby's need to preserve his mother's care taking functions when she is not there.

***

Lana, the very child-like patient I discussed earlier, who expressed her desire to be an elephant so her mother would never leave her, expressed her fear of losing me, her symbolic mother, during one phase of her treatment. She feared she was going to lose me because I was getting married. Her fear of loss was so great she stayed awake for sixty-five hours without eating while she obsessively crocheted a doll. The doll, it turned out, was supposed to be a facsimile of me. She was going to use it as a substitute for me. Lana was never soothed by her mother and therefore had never learned to soothe herself. Facing the prospect of losing me she literally created a transitional object hoping the crocheted facsimile of me would help soothe her as I did, when, as she feared, I was no longer there for her.

***

Gradually the child loses interest in this transitional object. The soothing functions of the Teddy Bear or "blank" become internalized; that is, they are taken into the child's own ego, so the object itself is no longer needed. Consequently, the child has within himself the soothing functions to replace what mother did for him when she rocked him to sleep, read him a story or otherwise reassured him.

Failures in parenting, however, interfere with a child's ability to take in and internalize these soothing and tension-reducing functions of a good-enough mother. That child, and later the adult, may compensate for this by deriving soothing and tension reduction through nurturing himself, *by eating.*

For the overeater, food or the act of eating itself, may function as a transitional object. Food is used then, unconsciously, to assuage the feeling of painful separation from mother. With food, the overeater is not only eating to nurture, but eating with the unconscious, symbolic wish of connecting with the soothing and the care taking functions of the mother. Food and eating, unconsciously, fulfill the function that the transitional object did in early childhood.

Eating to Comfort

*E*ating, *for some, magically comforts in the same way a Teddy Bear or "blank" magically soothes a child.* Eating derives its magic from its connection with mother and because eating is inherently satisfying and pleasurable. People who use food to comfort themselves have learned when they cannot soothe themselves, food can, although they are usually unaware of why it is such a comfort.

When people say they eat when they are upset, anxious or tense, they are actually suggesting the soothing function of their inner ego structure, which should be able to regulate their tension, is missing or not functioning satisfactorily. This lack may reflect that soothing which was provided by their mothers was insufficient, or that satisfactory soothing was provided by their mothers but was, for some reason, not adequately internalized.

When we have not adequately internalized the soothing functions of our mother we do not have an effective way to quell our anxiety. Lacking this internalized soothing function, we are likely to be overwhelmed with distress or anxiety when confronted with a painful situation.

If the soothing functions of our mothers are adequately internalized, when confronted with a painful situation we would feel distressed, naturally, but not be overwhelmed. We would respond in a self soothing manner similar to the way our mothers first soothed us and later our transitional object did. That is, we would comfort ourselves, reassure ourselves and calm ourselves down. Our internal mother would say, "This situation is painful, but don't worry. You'll be okay and things will turn out all right."

The overeater, whose internal soothing function is deficient or missing, uses food when he is overwhelmed with anxiety. Food and its connection to mother, feeling nurtured and being taken care of, serves as a way to soothe the distressed person.

Oprah Winfrey, who openly talks about her problems with overeating, was abandoned by her mother at a young age and left in the care of her grandmother. However her grandmother abused her and rarely expressed affection toward her. Oprah said that she felt she was a burden. Robert Waldron in his book *Oprah!* quotes her talking about eating pasta, "it's a comfort."[19] The language she used to describe her pasta love suggests the way she used food in the past: as something that comforted her, the way a mother of childhood or later a transitional object would. Because of her reported rejection by her mother, father and grandmother, we can speculate that she was not able to adequately internalize a "good enough" mother to have inside to soothe herself. She relied on food instead.

The actress Renee Taylor, in her book, *My Life On A Diet*, writes about how she had been overeating and dieting her entire life. As a child, she said, her father was rarely around. Her mother spent hours crying about her father not being around and about her own unfulfilled hopes of being a movie star. Renee Taylor said, "Food was my comforter and my best friend." She used food to reassure and soothe herself, because she was unable to rely on that comfort from inside herself.[20]

In her book, *Elizabeth Takes Off*, Elizabeth Taylor talks about how she used food to deal with unpleasant emotions such as the loss of privacy and the loneliness she felt when she was married to Senator John Warner, who was then campaigning for the Senate. She describes how she ate and drank without restraint to compensate for the pain of intense loneliness she was feeling. Ms. Taylor used food to soothe herself when her own soothing abilities failed.[21]

Fantasy

*F*antasies frequently relate to eating because eating is something a young child can understand. Also eating is an important part of the child's life. Childhood fantasies are often repressed for several reasons: because they may be too frightening to think about; because the fantasy does not fit into the child's moral code and would therefore evoke guilt; or because, as the child gets older, the fantasy does not fit his ideas of what can be done in reality.

For example, think about a six year old boy whose mother threw away his favorite toy because he hit his sister with it. He then has a fantasy of taking revenge against his mother. This would be an unacceptable thought to a six year old. Basically it would be very frightening because the child still desperately needs and loves his mother. To hurt her would mean to hurt and possibly lose someone whom he loves and who was necessary to his existence. In addition, the fantasy would be quite distressing because it would not fit in with the little boy's moral code and therefore would, if conscious, make the child feel very guilty. This type of fantasy would also be terrifying because of his fear of retaliation from the big powerful mother or father. So, as you can see, it would be necessary for this little boy to disavow these thoughts.

Distressing thoughts can be disavowed through repression, which means that even though a child or adult has these thoughts, they are no longer conscious. Therefore it seems to his conscious mind that they do not exist. However, although fantasies may be repressed, they can still exist in the unconscious part of our minds and thereby exert a great deal of power over our behavior and perception.

Linda is a good example. She is a woman who has repressed murderous fantasies towards her husband. He has been continuously abusive to her and she hates him. However she does not allow herself to acknowledge the depth of her rage, for she is afraid to feel alone. To her, on some level, someone is better than no one. So to protect herself from feeling anxious, she represses her fantasy of wishing to kill him. One morning her drunken husband threw the eggs she prepared for him in her face. This was a common occurrence when he was drinking, so Linda was used to it. As usual, she cleaned up the mess and got ready to do some errands. She got into her car and started driving towards the supermarket when she saw a traffic sign that said "Slow Down Kill." As it happens Linda passes this traffic sign every day on the way to the store. It actually says, "Slow Down Hill." But her unconscious fantasies broke through and distorted her perception. The result was her reading the sign as if it were giving a direction to kill.

Fantasy, be it conscious or unconscious, is ever-present. We daydream all the time, at least in one part of our minds. Unconscious fantasy can influence the way we experience and live our life. Jacob Arlow,[22] a famed psychoanalyst, states that unconscious fantasies, which are frequently of a primitive nature, press for gratification. He points out that the intrusion of the fantasy upon our perception may be so overpowering at times, as to be independent of reality. Fantasies are elaborated around certain childhood wishes and are a child's way of dealing with and adapting to his life. These childhood fantasies often persist throughout our life. They are frequently expressed in metaphoric terms. Childhood fantasies are the basis for the universal themes of myths, fairy tales and folklore.

Eleven

The Golden Fantasy

Sydney Smith, writes about a special kind of fantasy he calls the "Golden Fantasy." This fantasy is "the wish to have all of one's needs met in a relationship hallowed by perfection . . . . The wish is to be cared for so completely that no demand will be made except the capacity for passively taking in."[23] He states that implicit in this fantasy is the belief this experience, this state of bliss, was once attained, but is now lost. He speculates this fantasy is related to separation from Paradise, the all giving mother of infancy, and that some people spend their entire lives attempting to restore it. To those people, it is the central factor in their lives, and what influences their significant life decisions. These people are constantly searching for the "right one," the one who will be loving enough to make them happy.

Ironically, the person who maintains a "Golden Fantasy" often experiences no joy when the sought after closeness has been experienced with a spouse or lover. In fact the closeness is responded to as if it were a threat. It is the unconscious threat of being drawn back into that blissful union with mother only to feel reengulfed. The remerger threatens to blot out one's separateness and therefore one's existence. Those who harbor the "Golden Fantasy" vacillate between these two extremes. At one time fearing the merger and the loss of the self and at another time wishing for oneness.

***

You can imagine how it feels to be in a relationship with a person who maintains such a fantasy. This is commonly referred to as a "push-pull" relationship. It seems as if one moment he wants to be with you all the time, but a moment later he says he needs to stop seeing you because he needs "space." What has happened is the satisfaction of his wish for oneness resulted in his feeling engulfed.

There is another reason why these people refuse to accept the loving offering of the spouse or lover. To accept that love offering is to accept that the "Golden Fantasy" can never be realized. You might know of people who lament "that can't be all there is." Therefore the person may reject or let go of the loving other, only to continue the search for the one person who will, at last, fulfill him. In this way he can hold on to the fantasy that somewhere "out there" the person he fantasizes about exists. People who unconsciously cling to the "Golden Fantasy" frequently remember their mother as being unavailable.

***

Overeating is sometimes the unconscious expression of this passive fantasy of being completely gratified and not having to give anything back. Not only is the fantasy related to symbolically restoring the lost union with the all giving mother but also to the wish of not being deprived of anything. The feelings related to the lost bliss of infancy may even have some conscious elements, as in the thought, "why should I be deprived?" To eat only a certain amount of food is, to that person, being deprived. When that person gives in to the unconscious wish to be completely fulfilled and gratified, he eats.

Some people with this fantasy have a corresponding unconscious fantasy which occurs after a period of bingeing. After a certain time of bingeing they will fast. The fasting unconsciously represents autonomy and separation from the blissful union with the mother of infancy and manifests in the desire and ability to control oneself. By fasting, the person is demonstrating that he has control over himself and is accepting the limits of needs satisfaction.

Cannibalistic Fantasies

One powerful, frightening and guilt provoking, unconscious fantasy is a "cannibalistic fantasy." The unconscious cannibalistic fantasy can be related to intense oral sadistic rage towards another. This very primitive fantasy reflects the desire to destroy by ripping, tearing apart, chewing, and then completely devouring, the person who is hated. The devourer, however, not only hates the person, but frequently also needs the person. *With an unconscious cannibalistic fantasy, the devourer can have his cake and eat it too*. For, in this fantasy, the person who is devoured, exists within the devourer. This fantasy is one that is quite disturbing when conscious. That is why most people who harbor it are unaware of it.

Most people have a great deal of trouble acknowledging such rageful and primitive wishes. Just think of your reaction to the movie "Silence of the Lambs" when Hannibal Lecter's cannibalistic crimes were described. Most of us are repulsed and revolted at such disgusting primitive acts. Unfortunately, and extremely rarely, this fantasy, as revolting as it is, is not repressed, and is acted out. In the recent past we witnessed this grossly offensive, barbaric fantasy acted out in the crimes of Jeffery Dahlmer. He murdered many people and then cut them up and devoured them. God only knows what could bring about such horrendous acts of rage. However horrible when acted upon, cannibalistic fantasies are one example of unconscious fantasy in people whose overeating is related to rage.

It is important to understand that fantasies are not acts. Whereas the act of cannibalism is atrocious, the fantasy is not because a fantasy is just that, a fantasy, a product of one's imagination. Fantasies are not heinous acts; they are just thoughts. Individuals are often frightened when they become aware of unconscious fantasies, believing only a horrible person could have such awful thoughts. Actually the opposite is true. Aggressive fantasies are part of growing up and being human. We all were little once.

We all had angry feelings that were elaborated into primitive fantasies. Little children think in primitive ways. That is how we understand life, before we have the cognitive ability which allows us a more realistic understanding.

As adults we all get angry. Having rageful fantasies does not mean they will be acted out. Although you may have rageful destructive fantasies, most likely a stable moral code will prevent you from actually acting out these fantasies even if they were conscious. These fantasies are repressed because they are so frightening. Becoming aware of them can help us understand what they are about, and allow us to develop appropriate ways to deal with the rage which gives rise to them.

It is very important to realize thoughts and fantasies are not acts. You will be punished, and deserve to be, if you commit murder. You will not be punished, nor do you deserve to be, if you fantasize about killing someone. In the same way, if you have an affair you may be accused of infidelity, and may even be divorced, but no one can accuse someone who has fantasies about an affair of doing anything wrong. Often people who become aware of their unconscious fantasies are very upset by them because they have not yet differentiated between thoughts and deeds.

Aggressive fantasies are ubiquitous and part of being human. As a matter of fact, having fantasies may be very helpful in expressing wishes we would not otherwise want to express. Fantasies can allow us to feel more in control of ourselves through the expression of frightening feelings such as revenge, hate and anger in a manner that is not harmful.

Again, *Thoughts Are Not Deeds*. If fantasies are too guilt provoking, uncomfortable or likely to be acted out, it may be helpful to understand more about them through some counseling or therapy. The same holds true if you are using fantasies as a substitute for living.

Barbara

For as long as Barbara could remember she was angry at her mother. She was angry when she was young, because she said her mother gave all her positive attention to her siblings. Barbara was the oldest of six children. She was expected to "be good" and take care of her sisters and brothers. Barbara could not get positive attention from her mother by being good, because being good was what was expected. If she misbehaved, she was severely reprimanded and beaten. After all, she was the oldest; she should know better. It seemed that nothing Barbara could do would bring her mother's positive regard. Barbara said her mother even interfered with her ability to get attention from her father, telling her to leave him alone because he was busy or tired. She hated her mother for that.

When Barbara overeats, as we found out over time, she is unconsciously and symbolically, tearing her mother apart. She is ravaging her, chewing her, ripping her, gorging her and finally swallowing her. Ultimately, after the meal she feels satisfaction. She has satisfied her rageful feelings and has control of the meal, symbolically her mother, in the way she never had. In her fantasy she has incorporated her mother inside of her, and finally has her mother all to herself.

As an adult, when Barbara felt deprived, she would eat. But she wondered about the manner in which she ate. A current deprivation, such as not being invited to a party, would bring about a day of gorging on food. She believed she was feeding herself so she would not feel deprived. Yet her emotions while eating did not seem to fit feeling nurtured. Barbara, slowly became aware of the reason she ate alone and in such a ravenous, aggressive, primitive manner. What she discovered in her analysis, was that any current deprivation she felt evoked the unconscious feelings of rage and cannibalistic fantasies of childhood. Gorging herself was symbolically enacting a fantasy of what she unconsciously wished to do to her mother when she was little.

Her awareness finally allowed her to separate eating from her rage towards her mother. Now she is able to eat normally, express her anger more appropriately, and consequently have greater self esteem.

Thirteen

Filling the Emptiness

*M*any people overeat to fill up the feeling of emptiness inside of them.

Connected to fantasies of eating and devouring are fantasies of swallowing something or someone, so you can have it or them inside yourself. The feeling of emptiness often evokes the fantasy of swallowing, ingesting and taking inside oneself what is needed. A person may feel empty and alone because as a young child he did not have adequate "good enough" experiences to internalize. This empty and alone feeling can exist even when the person is in a room full of people. It is confusing and distressing when an intense feeling of emptiness occurs while sitting with a group of friends or family.

The feeling of emptiness is experienced as a painful sense of inner impoverishment of feelings, a feeling of deadness, boredom or superficiality. The cause of the feeling of emptiness may be multidetermined. That is, it may be based on one, but usually is based on several factors.

The feeling of emptiness may reflect the lack of a feeling inside of us of being loved by another. When we are children we internalize, take into our own egos, the experience of our relationships with the important people in our life, namely our mothers and fathers. When we enjoy a positive relationship with our mothers and fathers we experience, albeit unconsciously, an inner loving parent inside us. When that loving relationship is absent, we do not have it to internalize. Instead, what may exist, is the feeling of emptiness, signifying the absence of a good and loving other. The emptiness would, in this case, be perceived as missing someone or something, but being unable to fill the void, even when others were around.

The feeling of emptiness, a feeling of something missing, can result when our interactions with our parents are fraught with tension, displeasure, or worse, indifference. Rather than feeling loveable, smart, handsome, witty or experiencing some other positive, affirming feelings from our parents, we feel we are a burden, or stupid, or ugly or worse, invisible. We are, therefore, lacking and empty of positive internal feelings of worth. What is mirrored back from our parents strongly influences the way we experience ourselves.

It is possible that our actual parents did affirm us, but our perception of our parent's response was for some reason distorted and experienced as painful or neglectful. This experience may occur, for example, in the case of an infant who had a very painful illness. No matter what his parents did, the child felt no relief and continued to suffer. It is possible then, that the child perceived his parents as persecuting and neglectful because they did not take his pain away. In cases such as this, fantasies are sometimes elaborated about these misperceived "bad" parents. These perceptions, although misperceived and distorted, would be internalized as if those parents were not caring parents, because the infant does not have the cognitive ability to "know." The infant just "knows" what he experiences. Depending upon how long this situation continued and what kind of relationship existed at other times, would also influence how this situation would affect the child's inner world.

When parents and others mirror back to a child he is loveable, good, smart and handsome and the parent is enthusiastically interested in him, then the child internalizes those thoughts about himself. A child's self image is based on his inner thoughts and experiences. How the child perceives his parent's perception of him significantly influences his self image. Therefore, if a child's parents think their child is wonderful, most likely that child will feel that he is wonderful. He will not feel empty, because he will have an inner world of good and loving others. If a child's parents convey to their child he is a burden, the child will feel like a burden and may be prone to feeling empty. He will be empty of good and loving internal others.

Feelings of emptiness may also be a manifestation of guilt. Because we believe we are bad we feel abandoned and not worthy of any love.

Emptiness may also be a way for us to communicate dissatisfaction and resentment towards those who have not fulfilled our needs. We may complain about our feeling of emptiness to another as proof of the other's failure.

The feeling of emptiness may be an unconscious expression of our desire for, but lack of, a baby inside.

Many psychoanalysts believe emptiness is a defense against instinctual wishes. In other words, when we defend ourselves from being aware of our unacceptable instincts, such as feelings of aggression or sexuality, those feelings may be repressed. Consequently, instead of feeling the anxiety provoking forbidden rage or sexual longings, we experience an emptiness, a complete lack of passionate feelings.

When the feeling of emptiness exists, the fantasy of ingesting and swallowing what is needed may be invoked. This is related to childhood fantasies of being able to ingest what is desired. The person who feels empty eats to eliminate that painful feeling. The function of the eating is to fill the empty void inside. Afterwards a feeling of satisfaction may exist, because now, symbolically, he is filled with something good or wished for. Unfortunately, because the actual reason for the feeling of emptiness is not truly resolved, the eating offers only temporary satisfaction.

The Eucharistic rites of the Catholic mass illustrate, most dramatically, the idea of swallowing in order to take in the good other which is missing. P. Benoit, in *The Holy Eucharist*,[24] describes how the Eucharistic meal is not meant only as a symbolic action, but an actual eating of Christ's sacrificed body. Benoit says that in the Eucharistic banquet, in a mysterious way, we come in contact with and actually receive Jesus who died for humanity thousands of years ago. That by entering this sacramental contact we realize the gift of salvation. By swallowing the Eucharistic meal, the Catholic worshipers fills the void with the body, blood and goodness of Jesus Christ.

Overeating and becoming fat is sometimes used as a protection against inner feelings of emptiness and therefore vulnerability. In this fantasy, being fat, and perceiving oneself to be huge and impenetrable, eliminates the feeling of vulnerability.

Jackie Gleason dated his compulsive eating to the time his father abandoned him when he was eight years old. Jackie fondly remembers his father taking him to see a vaudeville show and silent movies. Watching people laugh at those times brought about his decision to be a comedian. Before he died he told a reporter the reason those shows made such an impression on him, was because he shared them with his father. W.J.

Weatherby's book on Jackie Gleason,[25] discusses Toots Shor, one of Jackie's best friends and the man who owned the drinking holes that Jackie frequented. Toots Shore said that Jackie could not understand how his father could leave him if he really loved him. He said his father's abandonment plagued him his whole life. Jackie Gleason's eating habits are infamous. One can hypothesize that eating was a way that Jackie Gleason attempted to fill up an emptiness caused by his father's abandonment.

Charles

Charles' mother was a very depressed woman who was unable to give him the positive attention every child needs. But she fulfilled her maternal obligations by feeding him well. She gave much thought to the home cooked meals she prepared for him and his father. However, other than taking care of his physical needs, she was not available to him. Their relationship was devoid of much emotion or interaction. Charles remembered coming home from school and seeing his mother either lying on the couch watching television or behind a locked door, holed up in her bedroom. Charles' father was a very angry, critical man. He considered himself a financial failure and a loser in his wife's eyes. In his relationship with Charles, it seemed that whatever Charles did displeased him. Although Charles was apparently a bright student, well liked by his peers and teachers, his father would call him lazy, stupid and ugly. Charles tried hard to please his father, but to no avail. It appeared that because his father was so unhappy about his own life, he displaced his anger onto Charles. In fact he seemed to be jealous of his own son.

Charles, with the strong support of some interested teachers, graduated from college and went into business. He was talented and lucky and became very successful. Nevertheless he was unsuccessful in one area; his weight! He couldn't stop eating. As a child and teen he was somewhat overweight, but not so much that he considered it a problem. He was an athlete then and very active, so he worked off the extra calories he ate. As an adult he was eighty pounds overweight. Although his weight upset him greatly, he could not maintain any control over his eating. When dieting he would lose twenty-five pounds. But then he would gain back thirty-five. When describing his eating he would simply say that he just loves to eat. It was one of his favorite things to do. It didn't matter what the food was; he loved it all.

Charles described feeling empty all the time. He ate, he said, to fill up what seemed like a bottomless pit. He always felt hungry, although he recognized that after a big meal his body was full. He described this feeling of emptiness as a painful, emotional feeling that had been with him throughout life. Even when he was with his friends or he was being honored with an award, he felt empty. It seemed to him that no matter what he did or experienced he remained unsatisfied.

Charles was eating to fill an empty inner self which was devoid of internal good and loving others. Even though he had an abundance of positive input from many people in his life, the lack of positive, affirming feelings from the people who were most important, his parents, made him feel empty. Because he lacked positive feedback from them, he identified with their perceptions of him and believed he was unlovable. He felt he was a burden, lazy, stupid, and ugly. Eating for Charles was the only way to symbolically swallow and fill himself up with his longed for fantasied good parents.

Charles' emptiness also served as a defense against awareness of his rage towards his parents. He was more or less empty of passionate feelings in general, but especially so of his rage. This defense protected him from anxiety related to his wish to destroy his parents and his fear of losing them. He felt guilty about his unconscious wishes, and his profound emptiness provided a deserved punishment.

Fourteen

Filling the Void

If you have become aware that eating symbolically represents supplying love, nurturance, soothing or filling yourself with positive things denied to you as a child, recognize eating is not actually fulfilling those needs. In fact, overeating may undermine gaining positive attention and acceptance, as frequently overeaters withdraw from activities where acceptance and loving nurturance may be offered. Eating may successfully soothe you or fill you up when you are feeling bad, lonely or empty, but that comforted feeling you get while eating is quite temporary. Afterwards, most likely, you will feel worse than you did before you dove into the food. Do the 10 minute exercise to forestall eating food that will divert you from your goal of being thin. Commit yourself to not bingeing or overeating for just 10 minutes; it is really a short time for a worthy endeavor. During that time contemplate ways you can genuinely gain the love, nurturance, acceptance and soothing that you are missing and for which you are truly yearning. Express these feelings to someone who cares about you. Think about healthy, realistic and affirming ways you can develop a loving and accepting atmosphere. Talk to friends and ask for their suggestions. If you are not comfortable doing that, consider joining a support group where talking about such things is the sole purpose of the group.

Realize the reason you were not loved and accepted as a child was not because you were unlovable; all babies are loveable. Unfortunately, for whatever reason, the circumstances in your childhood were not able to provide you with what you needed and to which you were entitled. Do not now do the same thing to yourself. Do not continue to treat yourself abusively and without love and acceptance. Recognize you must provide for yourself what your parents and family were unable to provide. Give yourself the loving, acceptance and soothing for which you yearn. Think about all the nice things about yourself. Do not devalue your attributes, rather recognize and appreciate them. Be a wonderful, loving and comforting parent to yourself. You can do it, I know you can. Plan to treat yourself to something special just because you are a wonderful person. You are unique and special and need to recognize that!

If you succeeded in diverting yourself from eating those foods which you had planned not to, you did a great job! GOOD FOR YOU! Give yourself plenty of recognition for your achievement. Reward yourself with something special for your accomplishment. Make sure not to devalue this victory. To someone who does not have a problem overeating it may not appear to be such a big accomplishment. To those of us who struggle with overeating, it is a triumph! Many of us are so quick to fault what we do or do not do, but have a difficult time recognizing our accomplishments, strengths and talents. Again, do not do to yourself what has been done to you in the past. It is bad enough you did not get the love you needed then. Do not deprive yourself of that love now.

If you were not able to resist eating those foods you hoped to avoid, you must not chastise yourself. Doing so is not only unhelpful, it is also destructive. It perpetuates the feeling that you "can't." That is not true. YOU CAN! Encourage and commit yourself to do better next time, and do so. The more familiar you are with why you are eating what you are, the better able you will be to control which of your wishes rule. Of course the wish to be comforted is a primary wish. However, refraining from overeating and acknowledging your ability to be in control of what you do, is truly quite comforting.

Fifteen

The Experiment

Being concerned about her friends' crash diets, a High School Senior, Juliette Lee Taska, performed a scientific experiment that resulted in finalist status in the prestigious Westinghouse science contest.[26] Ms. Taska invited 91 of her Lawrence Senior High School classmates to watch *Terms of Endearment,* a sad movie about the relationship of a mother and her dying daughter. The students were separated into two groups. Both groups were told Ms. Taska was studying food craving during the menstrual cycle. Snacks were put out for all. One group was shown diet commercials during the showing of the movie. The other group saw commercials unrelated to dieting. An intriguing result ensued. The group watching diet commercials ate twice as much as the other group. "It seems that diet commercials are a key factor in changing a person's mood and causing them to eat more. It's still a mystery why," said Taska.

We can speculate why now, knowing what we do about our unconscious thoughts and wishes. A stimulus suggesting the loss of nurturance, in addition to watching a movie depicting the loss of a loved one, most likely brought about the group's need to gain reassurance of sufficient nurturance by eating more.

Recognizing that unconscious wishes often prevail over conscious wishes, we know it is quite possible to gain weight when we believe we are trying to lose weight. Most of us who struggle with overeating know that experience first hand. Often, shortly after we begin to diet, we eat more than ever. We now know this accelerated eating, soon after the start of a diet or following the success of weight loss, is due to our unconscious wishes which stand in contradiction to our conscious desire to be thin.

The Log

An important step towards mastering our desire to be thin, is to keep a log. Keeping a log enables us to become increasingly aware of why we are eating when we are and what we are. Using any type of note-book, write down on one side of the page everything you eat including the quantity. This log is for your eyes only, so be truthful. On the other side of the page, next to the food eaten, write down <u>all</u> the feelings you had <u>before</u> you ate, and then <u>afterwards</u>. Since this exercise helps us develop more awareness about the reasons we eat when we do, it is a good idea to use this log a few days before you start a diet. Once you start a diet program it is essential to use this log for at least one month. It is especially important to keep this log when you are reading this book. You may find it valuable to read this book more than once, as the more familiar you are with the reasons many people overeat, the easier it may be to identify the particular reasons you overeat.

While keeping your log you may get in touch with thoughts and feelings before or after you eat that surprise you, that contradict the reasons you thought you were eating. Perhaps you will have thoughts such as "I'm entitled to pig out. They gave me such a hard time." Or, "If I continue to look this good no one will like me." Or, "I'm sick of being so 'good ,' I'm going to eat that entire chocolate cake." Or, "If I continue to lose weight it will be dangerous." It is good to identify thoughts such as these. Only through your awareness of them can they change.

The feelings and thoughts we have after eating often signify important ideas we have about being overweight. For example, feelings such as anxiety, satisfaction, guilt, anger, fear, etc., may represent significant clues as to why we are overeating. See if you can identify feelings and thoughts you have after eating and try to understand to what they are referring.

After you write down your feelings and thoughts about what and why you ate, spend time at the end of the day to think about those thoughts and feelings. It is <u>essential</u> to set aside time to do this. If you find yourself thinking I have no time to do this, it is indicative that a part of you still wishes to remain overweight. No matter how busy we are, we all make time for what is important to us. If we say it is important, but don't give it the necessary time, what are we really saying?

The best way to lose weight and maintain it is to eat only when you are hungry, and to stop eating when you are no longer hungry. It is also important to have regular meal times to avoid feeling famished, which eventuates in most of us overeating. However, eating is pleasurable. Sometimes we want to be able to eat just because we feel like it. We can do that, if we do it with the right foods, in the right amounts. With the advent of low fat foods, sugar substitutes, and nutritional facts posted on most foods, the 1990s is a better time than ever before to successfully diet and still be able to enjoy delicious food.

Nurturing ourselves means
being loving parents to
ourselves.

Part Three

To Be Or Not To Be, That Is The Question

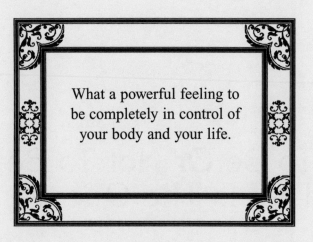

What a powerful feeling to
be completely in control of
your body and your life.

One

To Be or Not to Be,
That Is the Question

*T*here is a common, but <u>invalid</u> perception that all overeaters are
people who have no control over their eating. An overeater,
himself, may also believe that. To some extent it is true, because
the overeater is not in control of what is being directed by an unconscious
motivation. However, not all overeating is an indication of <u>lack</u> of control.
Sometimes, in fact, it is a manifestation of the opposite. Sometimes what
appears to be a <u>lack</u> of control, is in actuality, the unconscious wish to be
in control.

All human behavior is based on psychic determinism. That means none
of our behavior is accidental. All of our behavior is has meaning and
causes. But since unconscious processes greatly influence our behavior,
we may not be aware of what is determining a particular behavior of ours.
Nonetheless, all of our behavior is purposeful and goal oriented and based
on past events.

Fran

ran is a very bright and capable woman. She excels at her job
teaching elementary school children. She is charming, vivacious, a
stimulating conversationalist and a compulsive overeater. As she
tells it:

"I was always the 'good girl.' I was everything my mother and father
wanted from a daughter. When I was little, they wanted me to be good, eat
all my vegetables, have good eating manners, never put my hands in my
plate, never be wild or run around, be polite, be happy and smile, wear what
clothes they wanted me to wear, go to bed without a fuss. I did all that.

"When I got a little older they wanted me to eat all the food on my plate
(because people are starving in China), do my homework, get good
grades, never be fresh, say hello to the neighbors (even ones who hated
little kids), be friends with everyone, clear the table, brush my teeth after
every meal, wear the clothes they wanted me to, like whom they wanted
me to like, and dislike whom they didn't want me to like, be clean and
neat all the time, don't laugh too much, never cry, and never tell any of
the neighbors anything that was going on in our family. I did all that.

"In my teens they wanted me to eat all the food on my plate, be thin, have
the same opinions they had, not talk back, do well in school, don't have
sex, have lots of boyfriends, don't have sex, keep my room clean, don't
have sex, think they are the greatest parents, don't have sex. I did all that.

"When I got married they wanted me to do what they wanted me to do,
live where they wanted me to live, wear what they wanted me to wear, buy
furniture they wanted me to buy, cook the food they wanted me to cook,
invite over whom they wanted me to invite over and virtually, be like
them. I did all that.

"My husband wanted me to live where he wanted me to live, work where
he wanted me to work, wear what he wanted me to wear, and cook what

he wanted me to cook, and invite over whom he wanted me to invite and have the same opinions about everything that he did. I did all that.

"At work I needed to please everyone, especially the unnamed everyone's in my mind. I needed to be perfect in every way. I needed to be the best, most lovable and understanding teacher for my students and their parents. I needed to be the best teacher in the world for the administration. Mostly I had to be the best teacher in the world for that little voice inside my head that would tell me I'm a total failure if I weren't making everyone smile.

"Overeating and bingeing were the only times I did exactly what I wanted to. I felt when I binged that I was defying some authority. I ate as if I were saying to some enemy, 'Ha! Look I'm eating potato chips, pretzels, oreos, ice cream, candy, chocolate pudding, everything I know I'm not supposed to eat. And there is nothing that you can do about it.' I ate when I was not hungry. I ate things I didn't like. It was as if there was someone there with me whom I was covertly defying.

"I had to be in so much control throughout my life. I was always making sure to do this perfect, that perfect and everything perfect. People admired me because of how in control and perfect I was. They thought the only thing that was beyond my control was eating. But they were wrong. Even eating was within my control. In fact it was only eating that I was really in control of. When I was eating it was as if I finally had the control and ability to tell them all to go to hell. I would do exactly what I wanted to do and not what anyone else wanted or expected me to do. By bingeing, I was refusing to be perfect. By bingeing, I refused to be deprived. By bingeing, I refused to listen to what I should do or shouldn't do. By bingeing, I refused to listen to what anyone said is healthy or unhealthy. I just refused. Although I hated myself because I felt disgusting and fat, I needed to stand up to that unseen authority that lived inside of me."

Two

In Complete Control

*P*eople who overeat may be consciously or unconsciously behaving in opposition to what they believe they are supposed to do. Overeating becomes an expression of defiance of what is expected, what is right, good, healthy and so on. The desire to exercise our own will and the need to exert our autonomy may be motivations for doing the opposite of what we believe is expected of us. Expressing defiance in this way may be recognized and conscious, or unconscious and completely outside our awareness. When overeating is an expression of defiance it is as if the person is sticking out his tongue and chanting, "Na, na, na, na, na. I am eating all the foods I'm not supposed to eat and you can't do anything about it."

Unfortunately, although the overeater in this case wishes to defy and reject the standards of society or an individual, that wish does not eliminate the shame and self contempt the overeater feels. Even though the motivation for overeating may be rebellion and the attempt to be in control of one's own life, an overeater's resulting shame and degradation often makes him feel more vulnerable and less in control of his life.

***

Elizabeth Taylor, writing about the media and the world watching her "yo-yo" weight said that she rebelled against their comments by eating more. Her defiance and feelings of guilt and shame stood out as targets for everyone to notice and attack.[27] She wrote, that while others thought she was out of control, she was actually in complete control, knowing exactly what she was doing. She was doing precisely what she wanted to do: acting out her anger and defiance.[28] In fact, she says one reason she decided to write her book, *Elizabeth Taylor Takes Off*, is because she was so disturbed by the media referring to her weight gain as being due to outside forces she could not control. She insisted they know she was actually very much in control.

***

Speaking about dieting, an overweight woman says, "The whole idea of exercising control infuriates me. That's the image I hate about dieting and people who eat in moderation. I hate it as much as I hate the fat and the disgust. It seems so niggardly and pinched and puritan."[29]

***

One obese woman tells about her struggles to be "good" vis-a-vis her mother who was trying to help her lose weight as a child. She says she would try so hard to be "good" and then collapse from not being able to be good anymore. She would sneak food and worry about a confrontation with her mother. "My mother is very controlling about food generally . . . . I watch the rigidity with which she prevents my kids from eating. Partly because she wants her meal appreciated, partly because she wants to be in control of the stuff that's in her domain, partly because she has legitimate concerns about nutrition, and partly because food is one of the places where she expresses her very need to control the world around her . . . . For me fatness is the only area in my life where I've allowed myself to relinquish control, to be irrational and crazy, counterproductive, be rebellious against my family."[30]

***

Another woman states, "If the society has a horror of fat people and sees them as antisocial characters, who are greedy, secretive, isolated or self absorbed, then he or she comes to feel embattled with the environment."[31]

***

However, even with the shame, for some there is feeling of triumph. The overeater may be pleased that his shame is visible for everyone to see; for everyone to see the failure of the parents, especially those parents who are most conscious of appearances and worry about how things look to others. An obese child who is angry with his parents, can delight in knowing that his parents, through his reflection, are feeling the same shame that he is.

***

As one woman tells it: "I was in a therapy group and the therapist said,

'Finish the statement: The good thing about being fat is . . . .' I said the good thing about being fat is that it's obvious there is something wrong. It is a statement that something was wrong with my childhood, with the way my father treated me. There is absolutely no way to hide 300 pounds."[32]

***

I have been talking about people who behave in ways that are quite destructive to themselves, both physically and emotionally, as a way to express intense anger, rebellion and control. Because of the conscious or unconscious wish to defy some authority, some people behave in ways that often result in them feeling shame and humiliation. The self-destructive behavior of overeating, especially if it is extreme, frequently causes a reaction of repugnance from others. However painful that may be, the need to defy, express anger or demonstrate autonomy is so strong, that overeaters are willing to suffer the consequences.

What is all this anger about? Why all this rebellion? Why would someone behave in ways that hurt themselves just to express anger?

Three

Now I Have Control

In the beginning of life we, as infants, do things because of our impulses and needs. We eat and eliminate our bladder and bowels to achieve pleasure and satisfaction for ourselves. Our mother is experienced as that part of ourselves that satisfies our needs. Later, as we approach our second birthday, changes take place in the way we relate to the important people in our life.

In an earlier chapter I discussed the separation-individuation phase of child development, where we, as toddlers, begin to explore the world beyond our mother. This stage of life is a time of crisis and significant development for us. At this time we begin to be able to move around, take bold adventures and be more in charge of where we want to go and what we want to do. Our ego and thinking processes also mature around our second year of life. This brings forth a time of great crisis for us, for now we begin to recognize that we are not actually connected to our mother, that we do not truly share one boundary, that we are not merged at all with her. We realize that we do not share in our mother's perceived omnipotence. We feel vulnerable and scared.

This period of time can be quite distressing to us. Consequently this is a stage when others can note great vacillations in our mood. One minute we, as little tykes, seem elated and full of ourselves, as if the world is our oyster, and the next minute we are genuinely upset. Everything we thought we could do with impunity, like fearlessly climb on our mother's new table, we find is untrue when we fall and hurt ourselves. Our distress relates to a change in our perception. We realize we are not omnipotent and impervious to injury. We cannot do anything we want to and be okay.

We become increasingly aware we are actually separate from our mother and therefore, not in control of her. This is quite disturbing, for not being in control of our mother means that essentially we are not in complete control of our mother meeting all of our needs. Actually, that is the real motivation for anyone's desire to control another person. By controlling another person we can ensure all our needs will be met.

However due to our physical and mental development at this stage, we do gain control over our life we never had before. We can crawl or walk wherever we want. In the past we were completely dependent on our mother to know what our needs were and to take care of them. At this time, because we have begun to learn how to speak, we can tell mommy what we want and what we do not want.

Unfortunately at this time, we also discover mommy's needs do not always coincide with ours. And that becomes a problem for us. It evokes our intense feelings of disappointment and hostility. Before we thought our wish was our mother's command. Now, recognizing the truth of the matter is truly upsetting and enraging.

Another thing that happens around our second birthday is that our sphincter muscles develop, which bring about our ability to control our feces. This is an extraordinary accomplishment for us. We now have our own object, a fecal solid substance which we can feel and which gives us a pleasurable sensation. Now we have control over something that is ours, something we had not experienced before. We can hold on to this object or let go of it. We can do virtually whatever we wish with it.

It is difficult for us to relate to the notion of the stool being a prized possession. We have all (or at least the majority of us) been socialized to be disgusted by our bowel movement. But, alas, at one time all of us took great pleasure in our stools. We probably even played with them. But due to our proper socialization and defenses, all those feelings have been properly repressed.

Freud called this stage of a child's life the "anal stage," because the focus of pleasure is on the anus. That this object, this fecal mass, is quite significant at this stage, is confirmed by the fantasies that young children have about it.

As we begin to develop greater control over our bladder and bowels we are expected to be trained to do our duties (great pun intended) in the toilet. When we finally have complete control and autonomy over something of our own, our feces, we are expected to give it up and do what our parents want us to do with it.

Until now, we have experienced our mother as the provider of gratification of all of our needs. However, at this time, around our second birthday, our mother seems to respond differently toward us. We now experience her as the person who is imposing restrictions on our independence. She expects us to make in the potty. This new state of affairs brings about aggressive feelings in us towards our mother. Those hostile feelings undoubtably express, "Stay away from my special thing. I'll do with it what I want."

Deprivation and restriction inevitably evoke aggressive feelings. Now, however, we have the power and capability to express our aggressive feelings. We can do this through the control of our feces. We can now determine for ourselves whether we will or won't control our feces and "make" in the potty. We use feces as a gift, on one hand, and a weapon, on the other. If we make in the potty, it is as if we are giving our mother a gift. If we withhold it, we can use it to express our hostility. We finally have something we can use to express aggression, defiance or compliance: our feces.

At one time or another, most parents are actors in this kind of drama with their toddlers. The toddler tells the parent he wants to go "poo-poo," or go in the potty. The parents happily lead the toddler to the bathroom and put him on the toilet. And then they wait. But nothing happens. They encourage and cajole, but the child happily ignores their pleas to defecate in the toilet while he plays with whatever toy he brought along. Finally the parents give up. They take the child off the toilet only to smell, a few minutes later, the child's exhibition of his new power. He showed them who controls whom.

An interesting point in this regard: it is not uncommon for schizophrenic patients who have not achieved separation and individuation to give someone they like a package with their feces in it. It is given as a precious gift, a part of themselves. This reflects the primitive nature of the feelings of a child toward his feces before socialization.

***

The child during this stage of development is often heard saying "No!"; thus, the name the "terrible twos." He assumes an attitude of defiance as a way to affirm himself in his relationship to others. He tests out and practices his experience of new power. He practices this sense of power to consolidate his feelings about himself.

"No" means to the tyke, "I am in control, not you." "No" means, "I am a different person than you with my own thoughts and opinions." "No" means, "I exist and have power."

***

When we were infants our focus was purely on pleasure. By our second birthday our focus is more on strength, power and mastery. We can be seen exhibiting great pride in our actual accomplishments. Constructing a building with blocks evokes our great pride about being a talented architect. But when the blocks fall down, so may our mood. We begin to feel and reveal feelings of shame and inadequacy when our deeds result in failure.

Whereas as infants we wished for magical fusion with our mother, as toddlers we relate differently. Instead of wishing for reunion with our mother, we now wish to be like her. Besides striving for mastery and control of our world, we also want to be like the people we admire.

The positive aspect of our relationship with our parents and our desire to be a "big girl" or "big boy" and be like them, fosters our desire to control our instincts and aggression. When we enjoy a "good enough" parent-child relationship, our desire to be like our parents and to please them promotes our restricting our elimination to the bathroom. This decision, to be like mommy and daddy and use the toilet, like the big people do, brings about approval from our parents, which enhances our newly forming self image and self esteem.

"Look Mommy, look Daddy," are the typical words echoed by us when we have done our duties in the toilet and want to show off what a "big girl" or "big boy" we are. When we get praise for our "big girl" or "big boy" activities, we revel in it. When, on the other hand, our behavior meets with displeasure, we feel terribly deflated and ashamed.

Our parents' demand for us to use the potty are only one of many demands that are made upon us. As we mature and our capacities develop, more demands are placed on us. Where at one time we could happily play smearing our food all over our highchair and body, now we find we are told, "No." "No" is a word that means what we want to do must be stopped or it will make our parents unhappy. When we want to run in the street, we will hear "No." When we want to play with the electric wire, we will be told "No." When we want to eat the whole box of cookies, we will be told "No."

These restrictions and denials are not received very well by us. Any limitation or deprivation we experience is responded to with feelings of hostility. It is only by virtue of our positive relationship with our parents and our desire to please them and be like them, that our feelings of aggression are assuaged.

At this stage in our life we feel great ambivalence: feelings of both love and hate for our mother and the other important people in our life. This ambivalence is primarily directed towards our mother, since she is usually the one who sets the limitations on our activities.

***

It is essential that there be more loving and positive feelings toward parents than angry feelings, if these typical aggressive feelings are to be placated. If not, the child's aggression will predominate. The dominance of hostility will result in difficulties for the child that could possibly continue into adulthood.

These frustrations experienced by the child, however, do promote independent functioning. The child learns what he must do to live happily in his family. These are necessary lessons. He relinquishes his magical wishes of mother taking care of all his needs and he learns how to get his needs met by summoning positive feelings from mother and others. He learns that love involves giving as well as receiving.

However if the child's striving for autonomy is excessively frustrated, the emergence of hostile destructive impulses often result. If the positive feelings toward the frustrating person are not prevalent, and there is an abundance of hostility, great difficulties can be observed. Take, for instance, the matter of toilet training. If the training by the parent is either too severe or too early, the child will experience the mother as attempting to control his bowels, his free choice and will. This may result in either a hostile, defiant, ambivalent attitude, a regression to an earlier stage of dependency or certain personality problems.

Four

Defiance

Overeating is often a manifestation of a defiant attitude. Through overeating a person can say, "No"! "No, I will not eat what is good for me! No, I will not do what you tell me to. No, I will not be an obedient little girl or boy!"

Otto Fenichel, a noted psychoanalyst,[33] states the drive to amass wealth is connected to the anal period. Wealth, which symbolizes ones possessions, is sought to gain assurance that the individual will not have to relinquish his possessions again, as he once had to relinquish the breast and his feces.

Similar dynamics may operate for the overeater. Overeating, bingeing and the hoarding of food may express the desire to have and eat whatever and as much as one wants and not be denied anything. Clearly, overeating reveals an insistence on controlling, at least, one's body. If, as a child, a person was made to feel out of control of his body, later the adult may act to demonstrate that no one else will have anything to say about what he does with his body.

Overeating for many people is an unconscious way of angrily defying expectations of them. When overeaters eat for this reason, they make sure to eat everything they are not "supposed to" eat. You can overhear dieters speaking about their eating saying, "I was good today," or "I was bad today." Being bad means eating all the foods that they were not "supposed" to eat. Accompanying the statement, "I was bad," is often the feeling of shame or guilt for doing something wrong, very much the way the anal child feels when he soils. It is as if overeating is doing something naughty. In diet centers, a diet counselor personifies the inner person telling them whether or not they are good or bad, whether they are listening and complying to what they are supposed to do, or not. For many, having someone there who literally praises or disapproves of their eating is helpful. It harks back to the time the child felt so good pleasing his parents and so shameful when he did not.

Lack of satisfactory resolution of the conflicts of this stage may result in what is called an "anal character." Essentially, the anal character feels people are obstacles in his way. This thought evokes aggression and a constant need to defy some tyrannical constraint whose grip is experienced as an insult. The person fixated in this stage is unconsciously focused on the design of attack, devour, digestion and ejection.

In order to overcome the conflicts of the anal stage of development, the state of ambivalence, which characterizes this stage, must be resolved. During this stage the child vacillates between a trusting admiration of his perceived omnipotent parents and a disappointed, distrustful, depreciation of them. For there to be a positive resolution, the child must eventually be able to accept a realistic perception of the parents in which, hopefully, positive feelings overcome the negative, hostile, and derogatory feelings.

Bea

Bea, a thirty six year old woman, began therapy because her husband informed her he was repulsed by her weight. He was so revolted he refused to have sex with her. Bea came to see me ostensibly to get help losing weight. However, since the time he refused to have sex with her, she had not lost any weight; instead she had gained thirty pounds. She said when she married her husband she was approximately the same weight, "give or take ten pounds," as she was when he refused to have sex with her. This was enraging to her. Before their marriage he insisted he loved her, "body and all." She was approximately thirty pounds overweight then. She felt so happy to finally be loved by a man who totally accepted her.

Beginning therapy was, unconsciously, itself, an act of defiance. Clearly, she was giving her husband hope that she would lose weight by being in therapy, but actually, she was covertly defying him and instead gaining weight. His exasperation was met with indifference, because on another level she was really pleased with his response. It was a confirmation of the effectiveness of her expression of hostility. Bea married a man, who like her mother, always seemed to find fault with her. She responded to him as she did to her mother, with passive hostility and defiance.

Bea was using eating and getting fat as a way to "get back at" her husband. Consequently, she could not lose weight as long as he demanded she do so. Being fat made her feel ugly and ashamed. But Bea could not allow herself to become slim, because that would please her husband. Bea felt so enraged at her husband for consistently making her feel so miserable about herself, she sacrificed her own self esteem just to defy and hurt him.

As you may suspect, this was not the first time or first type of behavior Bea used to spite someone. Throughout Bea's adolescence she behaved in vengeful, defiant ways towards her mother. Her behavior was not just typical adolescent rebellion either. Her behavior expressed her rage towards her mother for criticizing and trying to control everything she did.

Ultimately, Bea began to understand the price she was paying for expressing her anger in the ways she did. She realized that she could express her anger in other, more constructive ways. Bea eventually was able to express her anger appropriately, by talking about it instead of acting it out. However, this did not change the way her husband treated her. Therapy helped her understand the unhealthy reasons she chose an abusive man, like her husband, to marry. Developing greater self esteem and the belief that she was entitled to be treated well by everyone, Bea ultimately left her husband.

A few years later Bea remarried a man who truly did love her body and all. Only then, because it was what she wanted to do, was she able to lose the weight she wished to lose and keep it off.

Five

Defying Overeating

The desire to express anger, defiance, and control are particular types of wishes connected to overeating. If you find your overeating is an expression of those wishes, you must develop healthier ways to express those feelings. Although eating may truly express anger, defiance and control towards people in our lives, look what it does to ourselves. Indeed, there are better ways to express these feelings without hurting ourselves.

***

What can you do if your eating is an expression of these feelings? The answer is simple: these issues must be resolved. Think about, write about, talk about your feelings of anger, your desire to defy, your need to be in control of your own life. Allow yourself to express the intensity of these feelings either alone or with someone you can trust. Shout, cry, express whatever strong feelings you have. Talk about it <u>a lot</u>. If possible share these feelings with the person(s) toward whom you are angry or from whom you need to wrest control. Recognize your wish to be thin is being sabotaged by these feelings, and become determined not to allow that to continue. Realize that you are giving the same people you are angry at the ability to control how you feel about yourself.

***

Before you eat something you will regret, give yourself <u>10 minutes</u> to think about it. Acknowledge <u>10 minutes</u> is not a long time; you can certainly be in *control of your body and eating* for that long. Remind yourself that you wish to be thin. Think about the fact there are much healthier and more effective ways for you to express anger than to be fat. Recognize you are the only one who can control your body and do not have to prove it by overeating. Understand that defying someone by overeating, is continuing to allow them to have power over you. If eating is the only control you have in your life, do something about that. Only you should be in control of your life. Become aware of what you can do to take charge of your life, and plan to do so.

If you succeeded by not acquiescing to your desire to angrily defy by eating, you did a great job. Acknowledge your success and give yourself the praise and reward you deserve. Recognize that by *not* eating you are now actually in control of your self and your body.

Six

Overeating to Please

S ome people overeat to defy. But some people overeat to please.

"A Mother's Creed"

"It's not fattening!
You won't gain weight!
Anything I cook for you,
Is perfect for your plate."

A Mother's love can erase
Those calories for sure
From all those gooey, fatty foods
That tempt us with allure.

"Now Mom, you know that I believe
All that you proclaim
I surely wish to keep you happy
   SO
We both will play this game.

I'll keep on overeating
To please you as I might
And will continue to make excuses
For my clothes that grow so tight."

For a Mother's creed is law
To all of us who try
And it matters not the grave results
Tho' inside we do cry.

— Diane Fero

Although it is not common for parents to want their children to be fat, this phenomenon does occasionally occur. A mother may insist she wants her child to be thin. She may even take the child to the doctor for assistance in weight reduction. But for some reason, unconsciously, the mother wants her child to be fat and sabotages her whenever weight loss is imminent. This need on behalf of a parent may be a manifestation of many things. One dynamic related to this situation may be the unconscious masochistic need for the parent to feel shame. Another may relate to attention the mother or parents get through having a child with a problem. Yet another may be the need to have the child close, controlled and not separated. A parent's envy of a beautiful child often results in that parent unconsciously influencing the child to be fat. Suffice it to say that many dynamics could operate to cause a parent consciously, or more typically unconsciously, to want his or her child to be fat.

***

A mother brought her sixteen year old daughter, who had a serious eating disorder, to my office to see me. The mother expressed great concern about her daughter's problem. However as soon as her daughter began to make progress and eat normally, the mother would fill the refrigerator with cakes and other fattening foods which her daughter found hard to resist. The daughter pleaded with her mother not to keep these foods in the house. But the mother refused, saying "That's your problem. You must develop will power. Why should I suffer because of your problem?" It was quite obvious the mother, unconsciously, had a need for her daughter to be fat.

***

In her book, *Such a Pretty Face, Being Fat in America*,[34] Marcia Millman writes about her interviews with women who belong to the New York City chapter of the National Association to Aid Fat Americans (NAAFA). This organization was started in 1969 by an average sized man who was married to an obese woman. He had seen his wife suffer the difficulties of being an obese woman in our society. Moreover, he endured the embarrassment of being a man attracted to fat women. The organization was meant to be a refuge for its obese members from a world that is hostile to obesity. The organization emphasizes social activities such as dances. But it is also a political organization promoting the belief that fat can be beautiful. Its intent is to bring about changes in how the public regards and treats fat people.

Men who come to the dances to meet fat women identify themselves as fat admirers. That is, men who have a sexual preference for fat women. Incidently, at these dances it is the heaviest women who are most desirable. Women who weigh under 250 pounds are less sought after. Some women in the organization are upset that men like them only because they are fat. In fact some men lose interest in a woman they are dating when she loses weight.

***

Investigators at the Mayo clinic[35] demonstrated that a major factor in certain children being overweight was their parents' unconscious wishes that their child be obese. When the parents gained insight into this phenomenon, through psychotherapy, the need for the symptom of obesity in their children was eliminated and the children's weight reduction followed.

***

In the novel *Lady Oracle* written by Margaret Atwood, the heroine describes well a child's confusion in the face of her mother's conflicted attitudes toward her weight loss.

"As for my mother, at first she was gratified, though she phrased it in her own way: 'Well, it's about time, but it's probably too late.' As I persevered, she said things like, 'You're ruining your health,' and, 'why do you have to go to extremes with everything?' and even, 'You should eat something more than that, you'll starve to death.' She went on baking sprees and left pies and cookies around the kitchen where they would tempt me, and it struck me that in a lesser way she had always done this. While I grew thinner, she herself became distraught and uncertain. She was drinking quite heavily now and she began to forget where she had put things, whether her dresses had been sent to the cleaners, what she had said or not said. At times she would almost plead with me to stop taking the pills, to take better care of myself; then she would have spasms of rage, a disheveled piecemeal rage unlike her former purposeful fury. 'You are the limit,' she would say with contempt. 'Get out of here, the sight of you makes me sick.'"

"About the only explanation I could think of for this behavior of hers was that making me thin was her last available project. She'd finished all the houses, there was nothing left for her to do, and she had counted on me to last her forever. I should have been delighted by her distress, but instead I was confused. I'd really believed that if I became thinner she would be pleased; a smug masterful pleasure, but pleasure nonetheless: her will being done. Instead she was frantic."[36]

Gloria

Gloria is a beautiful woman who was about fifty pounds overweight. Before she married Paul, she was a high school cheerleader, very popular and size eight. Paul was a football player and a very popular guy around school. But Paul was also very insecure and jealous. He always feared that he was not good enough for Gloria and that she would find someone better. Unconsciously, Paul tried to make himself feel more secure by sabotaging Gloria's looks and feelings of self esteem. He wanted Gloria to be completely dependent on him, so she would not leave him for someone else.

After they were married Paul would express annoyance and insist Gloria was neglecting him when she tried to do her nightly exercises. He would bring home all kinds of goodies and call her a killjoy if she did not want to partake in the bingeing of ice cream, cake and pretzels while watching T.V. When they went out to dinner he would cajole her into having several desserts, "because it was fun sharing," he would say. At home he would insist that she prepare all high caloric Italian meals; he explained it was how his mother cooked and what he was used to.

Gloria was gaining weight quickly and losing confidence in her appearance. However each time she went on a diet, Paul found one way or another to distract her from her efforts. One time her determination was so strong that his distractions did not work. She exercised and dieted and lost twenty-five pounds. Paul responded angrily saying she was boring and not fun anymore. When that did not deter her from dieting, Paul left her. He went home to his mother for several weeks. Gloria was devastated and frightened. She loved Paul and wanted him back. She feared losing him forever. They reconciled after several weeks of dating, which consisted of dinners out in nice restaurants and sharing many desserts. Gloria picked up and complied with Paul's unconscious message about her weight. Holding on to Paul was more important to her than being thin.

Since childhood, Gloria was fearful of losing those she loved. She dealt with that fear by giving up her autonomy and pleasing others instead of herself. "My parents only wanted what was best for me, so why wouldn't I comply?"

In therapy Gloria began to realize that she was compliant because she feared she would lose her parents' and husband's love if she was not. Her husband picked up on her fear and exploited it. To alleviate her anxiety about losing loved ones, she denied her desire for autonomy. Gloria identified with her husband when she dieted, believing she was a bore and a killjoy. This identification was used as a defense and protected her from angry feelings towards her husband for sabotaging her efforts to be slim. Recognizing this, she was faced with a choice: give up her autonomy or risk losing Paul's love.

For Gloria there was a happy ending. Ultimately she resolved her fears and became more independent. This impelled Paul to get some therapy for himself. Both of them eventually were able to be more independent and secure in each others love.

Seven

Prisoners of Childhood

A lice Miller, in her book *Prisoners of Childhood*,[37] describes people who relinquish their own feelings and strivings and adopt their parents' attitudes. These people have an emotional world characterized by a lack of respect for their own feelings. In fact they frequently have no idea what their true feelings are. They have a compulsion to control, which is the way they make sure their unacceptable thoughts and impulses stay suppressed. These are the people who are characterized as the "good girls" and "good boys" in their childhood.

Their backgrounds usually consist of a mother, who due to her own emotional insecurity, depended on her child to behave in a particular manner. The child manifests an amazing ability to unconsciously perceive and respond to the mother's needs. Doing so insures her love.

Miller states that this ability to pick up and respond to others' needs is then extended and perfected. These children become confidantes, soothers, and supporters of their own mothers. They virtually become mothers to their own mothers.

These people display what Winnicott termed the "False Self," revealing only what is desired of them. Usually the parents of these children approve of the child's false self, which leads to a bond with them that precludes autonomy. They dare not reveal, or more often even know, their True Self. This continues into their adulthood, at which time the person depends on others to affirm whether he is satisfactory or not.

An extreme of this is called the "as-if" personality. This term, coined by Helene Deutsch,[38] describes a person who relates somewhat as a chameleon. This person picks up others' needs and desires and literally becomes the wished for person. Because of this "as-if" quality, this person's personality may change depending on who he is with. If this person is with someone who would enjoy them more if they were gregarious, they are gregarious. However, the same person would be introverted and introspective with another who prefers those characteristics. Woody Allen depicted the "as-if" personality in the movie *Zelig*.

Eight

Pleasing Yourself

It is truly upsetting to recognize you are keeping yourself fat to please another. Hopefully, that recognition will foster your desire to overcome that need now.

The next time you are tempted to overeat, commit yourself to postpone eating for <u>10 minutes</u>. During that time think about what you are learning about why you overeat. If you fear you will not be loved if you become slender, it is essential you resolve that fear. Assess whether a basis for your fear actually exists. So many people fear that they will lose love if they become their own person. Many who have the courage to take the risk find their fears were unsubstantiated; that they were based on childhood experiences. Those who have the courage to finally take charge of their lives, ultimately believe that their lives are more important to them than the love of those who need to control them. No one's love should be worth the price of self contempt. In my experience, even those who seek to wrest control of their lives from people who threaten abandonment or withdrawal of love, when they finally do take back control of their lives, the abandoning person relents, because she or he needs the separating person as much or often more, than the person who is taking back control.

***

You should feel proud of yourself if you succeeded forestalling overeating, even if just for the <u>10 minute</u> exercise period. If you were not able to, commit yourself to do so next time, and do it. You deserve a big pat on the back and a reward if you were able to turn off the desire to overeat, recognizing what your eating was actually about and diverting yourself by using a more appropriate response. Make sure to give yourself both the praise for a great job done and a special reward. This recognition of a job well done is important. Don't dismiss it! Most of us are too ready to criticize ourselves for mistakes, but depreciate our need and entitlement of praise.

Part Four

"Oedipus Rex"

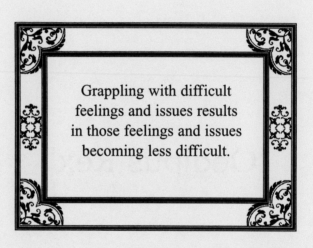

Grappling with difficult
feelings and issues results
in those feelings and issues
becoming less difficult.

One

Oedipus Rex

O marriage, marriage!
 The act that engendered me, and again the act
 Performed by the son in the same bed
Ah, the net
Of incest, mingling fathers, brothers, sons,
With brides, wives, mothers: the last evil
That can be known by men: no tongue can say
How evil!
> — Sophocles[39]

These are the words of Oedipus upon discovering he has unknowingly killed his own father and married his own mother. The very popular play, *Oedipus Rex*, written by Sophocles, was produced in Athens in 430 B.C.E. In the play, Oedipus, who grew up as the son of the king and queen of Corinth, was told by the gods he would "lie with my own mother" and "be my father's murderer." Although there were rumors in the kingdom of Corinth the king was not his real father, he fled the kingdom in fear of fulfilling the evil prophesy.

On his journey, he came upon an assaultive man whom he killed. When Oedipus reached Thebes he was confronted by the monster Sphinx which was killing all passers by. He became the only one to answer the Sphinx's riddle, thus saving the people of Thebes from the monster. In gratitude the people of Thebes made him their King. He married the queen, the widow of Laius, and had two sons and two daughters with her. Laius, the prior King of Thebes, had been mysteriously murdered ten years before.

A plague besieged the city of Thebes, which the gods said would be lifted only when the murderer of Laius is found. Oedipus therefore seeks the murderer. A seer, however, points his finger at Oedipus. The play unfolds with Oedipus struggling to discover the identity of the murderer and understand why the seer is accusing him.

It is finally uncovered that long ago King Laius and his Queen gave up their infant son, because an oracle from the gods prophesied their son would kill the King. The baby was given to a shepherd, who in turn gave the baby to the King of Corinth. The King of Corinth brought up Oedipus as if he were his own son.

Intent on discovering the truth, Oedipus coerces a shepherd into revealing that the man Oedipus killed on his journey years ago was Laius, his real father. The realization that he killed his own father and married his own mother, evokes anguish. Upon this revelation his mother commits suicide, and he blinds himself as a punishment for his evil behavior.

Freud discussed why *Oedipus Rex* had such universal appeal. "His destiny moves us only because it might have been ours because the oracle laid the same curse on us before our birth as upon him. It was the fate of all of us, perhaps, to direct our first sexual impulse towards our mother and our first hatred and our first murderous wish against our father. Our dreams convince us that this is so."[40] Although much criticism has been directed at Freud's interpretation of the play's appeal, Freud made Oedipus the most talked about man of the century.

Sophocles' play itself, contains a reference to the universality of these impulses in everyone's unconscious. When the queen, Iokaste, tries to reassure Oedipus about his fear of the god's oracle that he will sleep with his mother (whom they still believed was the queen of Corinth) she states:

"Have no more fear of sleeping with your mother:
How many men, in dreams, have lain with their mothers!
No reasonable man is troubled by such things."[41]

                                    ***

Freud developed the theory of the "Oedipus Complex," named after the play's tragic man, through the psychoanalysis of patients and interpretation of their dreams. His theory, which is generally accepted by most psychoanalysts, is the following. When a boy is around the age of three, he enters what Freud called the phallic phase. He begins to feel pleasurable sensations in his sexual organ. At that time, the boy begins to wish he were his mother's lover and desires to take his father's place with his mother. The little boy has been envious of his father's physical strength as well as his place in his mother's life. Now he perceives his father as his rival and the obstacle between him and his mother. Therefore, he wants to get rid of his father. However, he fears his father will retaliate by castrating him if he knows of these wishes. If the boy has seen a female's genitals, the possibility is verified, since to a little boy, a female's genitals look castrated. The threat of castration is overwhelming. In fact, Freud says it affects the little boy's entire relationship with his father and mother and later with men and women in general.

To protect himself from castration and retaliation at the hands of his father, the boy renounces his wish to be his mother's lover, and instead identifies with his father. Instead of feeling, "I want to take my father's place and be my mother's lover," the wish is transformed to "I want to be just like my father, big and strong and powerful." The wish to replace father in mother's bed is repressed, because it is too frightening a thought, and because the little boy also loves his father, and doesn't want to lose his love.

During this phase the little girl wishes to take her mother's place with her father. She is rivalrous of her mother's relationship with her father and therefore, has hostile feelings toward her. But as with the little boy, the girl also loves her mother and does not want to lose her love or incur her wrath. The girl, therefore, represses her wish to be the beloved of her father, and identifies with her mother. Instead of having fantasies of marrying her father she has fantasies of marrying a tall handsome man, just like her mother did.

Actually, as Freud acknowledged, all children have both positive and negative feelings towards both parents. A boy does not simply have an ambivalent relationship with his father and an affectionate one toward his mother. He also displays an affectionate attitude toward the father and a corresponding hostility and jealousy toward his mother. The same is true for the little girl.

It may be difficult to fathom that children have these intense sexual and jealous wishes. But recognizing children are completely dependent upon adults for their food, care and love, makes it easier to comprehend that anyone who interferes with fulfilling those needs will evoke jealousy and hatred. This situation is intensified as the child's own biological sexual strivings expand.

Two

Oedipal Wishes

Overeating may be a manifestation of unconscious oedipal strivings. Overeating can symbolize both unconscious forbidden wishes, and a punishment for those wishes, as well as a defense against them.

Unlike the tragic hero of *Oedipus Rex*, a seeker of truth, most of us do not seek all truths, especially truths which are genuinely disturbing. Despite the difficulties we have acknowledging some truths, they become undeniable when they are clearly apparent in dreams and fantasies. For example:

Jim, a thirty-eight year old lawyer, dreamt he was trying to seduce an older woman. A very big man came along. He knew if he continued, the man would hurt him. So he dropped his pursuit of the woman and became friends with the man instead. In this dream we see mother represented by an older woman and father represented by a big man. Dreams frequently express ideas the way the child perceived them. The fear of retaliation for the seduction of mother threatens the dreamer. The dreamer then decides to forget about the seduction and befriend the father.

***

Marlene, a forty-five year old woman, maintained a lifetime fantasy that her father really wanted to marry her. She believed he stayed with her mother only to protect Marlene from her mother's retaliation. Marlene held on to this belief despite witnessing her parents display affection towards one another. The fantasy protected her from feeling humiliated that her father chose her mother over her.

***

The reason most people were appalled at Woody Allen's affair with Soon-Yi Previn is because, although she was not his natural daughter, his affair with her is representative of acting out forbidden incestuous wishes. These wishes are taboo and are violently defended against. To see them acted out is disturbing to us.

***

Due to the distressing nature of these wishes, most people repress and thereby, disavow them. It is one reason why many disparage Freud's theory of the Oedipus Complex. These impulses are repugnant to us, and therefore we wish to repudiate them. Some people, however, do not repress these wishes completely. Although the memories are accompanied by anxiety and guilt, some people do remember wishes of wanting to be their parent's lover and experiencing the other parent as an obstacle and a threat.

***

John, a forty-five year old physician, remembers sleeping with his mother when his father was away on business. This occurred between the age of three and six, right in the midst of his oedipal phase. He remembers feeling sexually stimulated lying in bed with his mother, enjoying touching her breasts. When his father came home he felt rage towards him for displacing him and towards his mother, whom he experienced as a betraying lover.

***

Rose, a thirty year old business woman, remembers pretending as a child, that she was her father's wife. Using her play kitchen she would "cook dinner" for him when he came home from work. In fact, she remembers pretending to give birth to her father's baby. Connected to this wish, Rose elaborated many fantasies of getting rid of her mother.

***

Sandy, a six year old girl, was brought in to see me because she was having bouts of regurgitation. She symbolically demonstrated her oedipal wishes in play therapy. In our first session she began to play with the doll house in my office. She purposefully placed the Mommy doll and the Daddy doll in the bed in one of the bedrooms. Then she placed the girl doll in a bed in another bedroom. "It's bed time," she said as she placed the dolls in their appropriate beds. Suddenly, she threw the Mommy doll out of the bed and replaced it with the little girl doll, so the little girl doll was in bed with the Daddy doll. "You're not sleeping with him anymore," she emphatically said to the Mommy doll. "From now on, I am sleeping with Daddy."

Her bouts of regurgitation were symbolically getting rid of, purging, these frightening wishes. However, the symptom also represented a fantasy of fulfilling those wishes, as her mother was throwing up because she was pregnant, and had Daddy's baby inside of her. That significance to her purging was conveyed by Sandy when she placed the basinet, for the newly arriving baby, in the dollhouse bedroom, where she decided she and her daddy would sleep. Her fantasy was clear, this was going to be her and her daddy's baby. Her mother's recent birth of a baby sister stimulated her sexual wishes and anxiety.

***

Undoubtedly, oedipal strivings evoke very uncomfortable feelings for all children. Wishes to get rid of one parent, so we can take their place with the other, evokes anxiety and guilt. We fear retaliation and loss of love. And, although we have aggressive feelings toward one parent, we also love that parent and therefore do not want to lose him or her.

This phase of development is frustrating and often mortifying because in a healthy environment, reality reveals we cannot really replace one parent in the other's eyes. It can be profoundly painful to us, as children, to recognize our parents have a relationship with each other from which we are excluded.

Due to these intense feelings and the need for our parents' love, oedipal strivings are usually renounced and repressed. Those who unconsciously cling to the strivings of the Oedipal Complex, develop symptoms which interfere with their optimal functioning.

Symptoms that result from unresolved oedipal wishes are multitudinous. They range from difficulties in sexual relationships, to hysterical symptoms, to anxiety disorders, to obsessive compulsive disorders, to phobias, to difficulties in succeeding and to *overeating*.

Laura

"The Girl Who Couldn't Stop Eating"[42] is a paper that Robert Lindner, a psychoanalyst, wrote about a patient whom he treated. This is how he described her appearance after one of her eating binges. "Laura had two faces. The one I saw that morning was hideous. Swollen like a balloon at the point of bursting, it was a caricature of a face, the eyes lost in pockets of sallow flesh and shining feverishly with a sick glow, the nose buried between bulging cheeks splattered with blemishes, the chin an oily shadow mocking human contour; and somewhere in this mass of fat a crazy-angled carmined hole was her mouth."[43]

This was how this woman appeared after being overcome by an overwhelming compulsion to gorge herself. She described herself at these times as being ravenous, insatiable, eating until the point of "utter exhaustion," until her "distended insides protested with violent pain,"[44] until her "strained senses succumbed to total intoxication."[45] The tormented horror and degradation of these episodes were not to be believed. Laura described these fits as coming out of nowhere. One minute she felt fine, gay, busy, loving life and people and the next minute she felt she was on the way to hell.

She stated: "'I think it begins with a feeling of emptiness inside. Something, I don't know what to call it, starts to ache; something right in the center of me feels as if it's opening up, spreading apart maybe. It's like a hole in my vitals appears. Then the emptiness starts to throb at first softly like a fluttering pulse. For a little while, that's all that happens. But then the pulsing turns into a regular beat; and the beat gets stronger and stronger. The hole gets bigger. Soon I feel as if there's nothing to me but a vast, yawning space surrounded by skin that grabs convulsively at nothingness. The beating gets louder. The sensation changes from an ache to a hurt, a pounding hurt. The feeling of emptiness becomes agony. In a short while there's nothing of me, of Laura, but an immense, drumming vacuum . . . . The moment I become aware of the hole opening inside I'm terrified. I want to fill it. I have to. So I start to eat. I eat and eat . . . everything, anything I can find to put in my mouth. It doesn't matter what it is, so long as it's food and can be swallowed. It's as if I'm in a race with the emptiness. As it grows, so does my hunger. But it's not really hunger, you see. It's a frenzy, a fit, something automatic and uncontrollable. I want to stop it, but I can't. If I try to, the hole gets bigger, I become idiotic with terror, I feel as if I'm going to *become* nothing, become the emptiness . . . get swallowed up by it. So I've got to eat.'"[46]

Laura would eat until she was unconscious. She compared it to a state of drunkenness. Her father was often drunk when he lived home. He left her and her family when she was a child. Her mother was crippled and confined to a wheelchair. In a way, these states of being, while gorging, resulted in her becoming like both of her parents, crippled and drunk.

In addition to her problem with uncontrollable eating binges, Laura realized she was terrified of sex. Her fear of intercourse was interfering with her having satisfying relationships with men. A dream of hers illustrates that her fear of sex functioned as a defense against her unconscious wish to take her mother's place with her father.

She dreamed that a man was going to give her a gynecological exam. She was very frightened. He was examining a woman who was "'sitting or lying in a funny kind of contraption with all kinds of levers and gears and pulleys attached to it. I knew that I was supposed to be next, that I would have to sit in that thing while he examined me.'"[47]

In the dream, the man was going to do something sexual to her. She connected the gynecological contraption to her mother's wheelchair, thereby expressing her wish to be next in the place her mother was in. (Dreams are frequently disguised wishes.) Her sexual fantasies about her mother and father and her wish to have sex with the man, symbolically her father, are expressed in the dream.

Following the dream, she remembered how much she hated her mother and that she blamed her for her father leaving. About her father she said, "'Even when I was small, he was no good, no good to her and no good to us. But I loved that man. I could hardly wait for him to come home. Drunk, sober . . . it didn't matter to me. He made a fuss over me and that's why I loved him. She said I was his favorite: I guess I was. At least he made over me more than the others.'"[48]

Ultimately, Dr. Lindner discovered what brought about Laura's "fits" of eating. He witnessed Laura again after one of those uncontrollable eating episodes. Her face again looked distorted, but this time there was something different. From the middle of her body was a bulging arc, as if she were pregnant. Laura in her intoxicated state looked down and said, "'Baby-Looks-real-this way.'"[49] Laura had a pillow strapped to her body with adhesive. "'I-want-a-baby'" she said. Talking about the contrivance she made to simulate pregnancy she said, "'I guess I have to mike a new baby every . . .' Her hand went over her mouth. 'My god! Did you hear what I just said?'" Mike was her father's name. The reason she gorged uncontrollably was finally understood. She was attempting to fulfill her unconscious wish of having her father's baby. Lindner ends his paper saying, "It was for this impossible fulfillment that Laura hungered . . . and now was starved no more . . . ."[50]

Laura's case provides an excellent example of how becoming fat can be an expression of an unconscious wish to be pregnant. The wish has to be denied because it is a forbidden incestuous wish. The wish to have one's father's baby is so reprehensible and frightening that it is repudiated. However, at times, the wish is not completely renounced, but exists in the unconscious, longing to be fulfilled. When this occurs, a compromise formation, that is a symptom, often represents the struggle to express the wish and to keep the wish hidden. In Laura's case, it was her uncontrollable binges, her fear of sex and symbolic pregnancy.

Three

Resolution or Not

Promoted by the fear of retaliation and the wish for our parents' love, we identify with our parents moral code toward the end of the oedipal phase. To do otherwise is just too distressing. What occurs is a gradual internalization of our parents' prohibitions into our own mind. So even when our parent is not present, these prohibitions continue to exist. Now we hear our own inner voice say, "I shouldn't have done that. I'm a bad person for doing that." We respond to our inner voice's negative judgement with feelings of guilt. This is a new development. We no longer need our parents to tell us when we are doing something wrong. Our parents need not even be there for us to feel bad about our misbehavior. This new development is a profound one. It is the development of a structure of our mind. Freud termed it the "superego." We commonly refer to it as our conscience.

Trauma in a child's life may interfere with the resolution of oedipal strivings. If, for instance, a parent is seductive towards the child, the intensity of excitement may be beyond the child's ability to control. Consequently, the child may be unable to effectively repress incestuous wishes. Furthermore, since the child is unable to discharge the feelings of sexual excitement, these feelings may be experienced as painful, frustrating and confusing. Moreover, sexual excitement would be associated with danger, due to the fear of retaliation of the other parent. These feelings may color how this child experiences love and sexual relationships as an adult.

Frequently, people who themselves have not resolved the issues of the oedipal phase, reenact those strivings when they become parents. A mother who has not resolved her oedipal strivings may be seductive towards her son. A father who has not resolved his oedipal strivings may be seductive and show preference to his daughter. At times, these unconscious wishes are so intense that the parent reenacts the oedipal complex with the child of the opposite sex, by maintaining a hateful relationship with the spouse and a loving, adoring, admiring and seductive relationship with the child. This behavior is incredibly destructive to the child. The child experiences the parent's unconscious sexual feelings toward her and it evokes her own feelings of sexual arousal, which often results in the child being unable to have a normal sexual relationship as an adult, because incestuous feelings are associated with sexuality.

Unfortunately, this kind of situation can occur without the parent being consciously aware of it. If someone, such as the spouse or therapist, suggests to this parent that he is behaving inappropriately with the child, the parent often responds by saying that the person making this accusation has a sick mind and that he is only being affectionate.

***

Connecting her overeating with her father's wanting her to be a "hot number", a woman says, "I use to eat a lot when I got attention from men. Whether their response was positive or negative, as long as it was a confrontation with men, I'd start eating. When I was dieting, as soon as people would compliment me about how I was looking I would start eating . . . . And when I feel like a fat person it has to do with men and my relationship to them not food."[51] Overeating was the way this woman protected herself from the anxiety provoking feelings she had about sexuality. Sexuality represented to her being with her father.

***

At times, the oedipal wishes between parent and child are not controlled and are literally acted out. Unfortunately, this happens far more than most people are aware of. In the hope of stopping such child abuse, the media and social service agencies are attempting to make people more aware. I will speak more about actual incestuous relationships later.

***

A feeling of oedipal triumph may be experienced by a child when the parent of the same sex dies. It is as if the wish to get rid of that parent and have the other parent to oneself, has been fulfilled. This can create intense feelings of guilt and feelings of omnipotence. A divorce can affect the child in the same way. These traumas can exacerbate the anxiety of the oedipal phase and make its resolution more difficult. Difficulties in the resolution of the oedipal phase of development can reverberate throughout life.

Some people who have not adequately resolved their oedipal drama relate to any success as if it were an oedipal triumph. Unconsciously, they equate attaining their wishes with defeating their rival and obtaining the incestuous love of the parent. Consequently, these people often punish themselves for their success or sabotage it completely.

Jane is a woman who could not be successful for that reason.

Jane

Jane is a forty-five year old divorced, overweight woman who consistently undermined her success. The promotional exam she took at work is a good example of that. She knew the job completely, but office procedures necessitated passing an exam. For one month before the exam she would talk about the fact that she should be studying. But whenever she sat down to study, she became distracted. The week before the exam she did try to study. But by that time there was so much to study she felt overwhelmed and would fall asleep. The day of the exam she was frantic. She was so anxious, it was difficult for her to concentrate. Needless to say, she failed the exam. This phenomenon was not new to her. It was what brought her into therapy in the first place.

Jane grew up in a home with a "handsome, charming and successful" father. Her mother was described as being very pretty, but extremely dependent. "Working was something that lower class women did," her mother would say. However, her father did not respond that way to the women with whom he worked. It seemed to Jane, her father liked "the girls" and admired the jobs they did.

Jane secretly harbored her own ambitions. She wanted to be like one of the women with whom her father worked. Her conscious fantasy was that she would be a successful working woman and that someone like her father would fall in love with her. Unconsciously, she desired her father, himself. This was revealed not only in dreams, but also in fantasies and memories.

As a child and a teenager, Jane remembered fantasizing that her mother would be stricken with a fatal illness. In the fantasy she is quite distraught, but she takes care of her father and her younger brother. Eventually she, her father and brother move into their own home and "live happily ever after." The fantasy then becomes modified and her brother becomes her and her father's child.

Unconscious guilt about her oedipal wishes dominated Jane's life. In one therapy session she described shopping for a dress for a party. Instead of shopping for the prettiest dress she could find, she realized she was shopping for a dress that was not "too" attractive. This realization was astonishing to her. She thought about why she would want to buy a dress that was not "a knockout." Analysis revealed that couples she knew were going to be at the party. She feared if she looked great, she would be irresistible to the husbands and their wives would hate her and retaliate. On another level, she realized that was her secret wish: to "knockout" the wife and replace her in her husband's affections. Because this wish was so repugnant to her, she defended against it by making sure she would not look too appealing.

Jane's unconscious fantasy of an oedipal victory was so intense, she had to continuously defend against its actualization. Being fat was her defense. Being fat expressed, "I don't have any wishes to steal your husband. Look, I'm not even attractive enough to do that." Although she loathed the way she looked, she felt safe. Safe because she believed she was sexually repulsive. She could not seduce a man because she would not want him to see her body.

Her guilt over unconscious wishes resulted in depriving herself of what she wanted. She believed she shouldn't outdo her mother, therefore, she could not be successful or be happily married. Unconsciously, these things represented an oedipal victory.

Although occasionally she was involved in sexual liaisons, she was not orgasmic or able to experience pleasure in a sexual relationship. Her inability to be successful or enjoy sex and relationships with men, functioned both as a defense and a punishment, preventing her from being a "winner" and also serving as a punishment for forbidden wishes.

In time, Jane came to understand what was causing her unhappiness. She was virtually punishing herself for wishes all children have, but wishes which, for many reasons, she was unable to renunciate and resolve. She was able to understand that she was not committing a sin wishing to be with her father and wanting to get rid of her mother, because wishes are not deeds. Jane realized that she was not "bad" and deserving of punishment, and that she had a right to happiness and success. Ultimately, she was able to separate early childhood incestuous wishes from wishes to be loved by a man she admired. Jane was finally able to lose the weight she desired and feel free to be a sexual woman.

Four

"Chocolate Is Something You Have an Affair With"

Walter W. Hamburger, a psychiatrist, studied the meaning of food and eating in dreams his patients had. From his research, he concluded that food and eating in dreams are frequently symbolic substitutes for sexual feelings. His research corroborates other studies on food and eating in dreams. Hamburger believes that when sexual hungers are too threatening, they are displaced and substituted for, by a more acceptable hunger, food.[52]

***

Harvey J. Schwartz, a psychoanalyst, says the central wish of a person suffering from Bulimia, an eating disorder consisting of bingeing and purging, is the wish for incestuous impregnation. He states the anxiety and guilt over sexual fantasies, result in a regression away from sexuality, and induce bingeing and purging.[53]

***

Although being fat is emotionally and physically distressing, an individual who has unresolved oedipal conflicts may unconsciously choose to be fat rather than be sexual, for sexuality, in this case, would be connected to incestuous fantasies. Overeating can function as a sublimation, that is as a transformation of a prohibited impulse to a more socially acceptable form. Instead of acting on the wish of incestuous sexuality, a person may eat.

***

A woman talking about her compulsive bingeing says: "'When I binge it's like masturbating, shameful and forbidden. Each morsel I eat is more and more pleasurable, until the pleasure reaches a crescendo of ecstasy.

Afterwards, I feel exhausted and go to sleep.'"[54]

***

Another woman states: "'Chocolate is something you have an *affair* with.'"[55]

***

When the plumber noticed her hidden ice cream and chocolate, another overweight woman said, "' . . . I felt as if my husband had just walked in and found me in bed with our next door neighbor.'"[56]

***

"'Like lovemaking chocolate has it's subtleties. One kiss comes to you shrouded in plain silver foil, another emblazoned in royal blue and gold. Some kisses fade like childhood on your mouth, while others quiver with dreams not yet conceived. Some chocolates, like some love makings, give you a quick heady rush and let you down before you come out the other side. Others, of both categories, allow you to build to a gradual climax, with glimmers of ecstasy along the way, until a final cry is reached and you sink into the shadow of the moon.'"[57]

***

No one can deny that eating clearly reflects the sublimation of sexual desire for these women.

Five

Allowing Ourseves to Be Sexually Desirable

Wishes that are harbored in our unconscious are inevitably anxiety provoking when we become aware of them. If they were not anxiety provoking, we would have no need to keep them unconscious. Wishes related to sexuality, especially forbidden sexuality, are among the most anxiety provoking thoughts we have. Most people who keep themselves fat to avoid being sexually desirable, usually have some conscious knowledge of that. Often, what they are not aware of is the reason they wish to avoid sex.

Becoming more aware of the reason for avoiding sex can be upsetting. It is absolutely essential to remember that no thought or wish we have is bad. Every child harbors wishes which may seem deplorable to us as adults, and we all have remnants of those wishes. We are usually not aware of those wishes, because we deem them unacceptable and repress them. Each of us as children, had sexual desires for our parents. That is not bad or disgusting; it is part of normal childhood development. We repress these feelings because of how anxiety provoking they are and how dangerous they seem. The remnants of those repressed unresolved feelings affect many people in their adult life. Acknowledging those wishes is not immoral or bad. In fact it is good. Why good? Because only then can we possibly understand how those wishes are affecting our lives. Only then can we do something about our repressed wishes adversely affecting our lives.

***

If being fat is serving as a protection against sexuality, the fears associated with sexuality must be resolved. We must recognize and separate our sexual wishes connected with forbidden lovers, from sexual wishes towards people with whom it is healthy to have a sexual relationship. We can allow ourselves to be thin and sexually desirable by recognizing that the person we want to attract is not the forbidden lover of our unconscious wishes.

To do this requires deliberately thinking about it until it is no longer anxiety provoking. Think about how you, as every other child, must have wished to be the lover of your parent. Acknowledge that this was healthy and normal. Recognize how remnants of those wishes are interfering with your life today, because you are presently mixing up suitable lovers with incestuous lovers. Work on distinguishing and differentiating them so it no longer feels dangerous to be sexually attractive.

Some people mix up any triumph and success with incestuous wishes. To them, a victory is equated with defeating one parent and winning the love of the other. To be slender and beautiful may unconsciously mean triumphing over mother and being the winner of father's love. Being slender must be disentangled from this unconscious drama. It is not bad or wrong to wish to be slender, the prettiest, prettier than your mother or anything of the sort. We all want to be as beautiful as we can be. We all have competitive wishes. These are not bad, they are normal. Becoming slender and more beautiful is not, in actuality, stealing one parent from another.

***

Use this awareness and your thoughtful work, when you are doing your <u>10 minute</u> exercise to avoid disrupting your diet. Remember being thin and sexually attractive is healthy and good. Separate your childhood incestuous wishes from normal sexual desires, so you no longer have to shut down your sexual and beautiful self. Being slender and sexually desirable is something we are all entitled to be.

***

Once again, if you have succeeded in putting off your desire to eat that fattening food, praise and reward yourself. You did a great job! Keep up the good work.

Part Five

The Evil Eye

There is a green-eyed
monster out there!

One

The Evil Eye

Growing up I enjoyed a close relationship with my aunt, my mother's sister. She was the matriarch of our extended family. When I gave birth to my first child, she told me to put a red ribbon on the baby's crib for good luck. Since I was not superstitious, I was reluctant to do so, but she was insistent, telling me the red ribbon would keep away the evil eye. "What is the evil eye?" I asked. She could not believe my naivete when she told me that the evil eye is the sinister wish of people who are jealous. The only way I could protect my baby from the power of those wishes was to put a red ribbon on the crib, she said. She could not explain how the red ribbon would protect my baby, but assured me that it would. I laughed and said I did not believe anyone's wishes could hurt my baby and refused to put the ribbon on the crib.

Years later, when my children no longer needed a crib, I took it apart for storage. Lo and behold, there under the mattress was a red ribbon. She must have put it there when I was not looking. I laughed and affectionately thought about the good wishes and fears of my aunt. Or I wonder is it possible it was the red ribbon that protected my children? Nah!

***

The belief in the "evil eye" goes back to, at least, early biblical times. The belief was that some people could produce malevolent effects on others just by looking at them. The power of the "evil eye" is activated, according to folklore, when jealousy towards more fortunate people is aroused. Biblical narratives are replete with stories about the "Evil Eye." In the bible Sarah casts an "evil eye" on Hagar, Joseph's brothers cast an "evil eye" on Joseph, and Og the giant casts an "evil eye" on Jacob.

***

These admonitions about the "evil eye" may seem silly to you, but in many societies people who fear envy hide what they have. In many Latin America countries women do not acknowledge their pregnancy until it is obvious. This is based on a superstition that bragging could adversely affect the fetus.[58]

***

In the winter, Eskimos hide the best pieces of meat, before guests arrive, to avert envious eyes. In the summer, because the cooking is done outside and the food cannot be hidden, they feel obliged to share everything.[59]

***

In India the "untouchables," a caste of people who are born to low status and deprivation, are thought to have an "evil eye." Indians believe the person with the "evil eye" has the power to harm. In Ethiopia, similar power is attributed to the Buda, a class of people who also have low status and are quite poor. It is understandable that people with status and affluence might think those who have little or nothing, would be envious.[60]

***

In various cultures and societies throughout history, different methods have been designated to ward off the "evil eye." The color red seems to have significance as a measure to counteract the "evil eye." As with my aunt and people of Eastern European descent, red ribbons are believed to be effective. In Italy, the Tuscan ox wears a red ribbon between its eyes to protect it from the "evil eye." Painting their doors red or hanging red chilies on the door are ways that some people from Italy protect themselves.[61]

***

Many superstitions are connected with warding off the "evil eye." Spitting, throwing salt over your shoulder, wearing charms and amulets are all used as protection. Jewish people say "kayn aynhoreh," when giving a compliment or commenting on good fortune. This is to assure the person complimented, one is not envying him. The phrase idiomatically means "I will not cast an evil eye."[62]

***

Americans, possibly more than any other society, seem to be less afraid of the "evil eye." We show off what we have. We drive big cars and boats. We live in big houses with picture windows. We wear designer clothes to indicate how much money we have spent on something. However, what many Americans do to protect themselves from envy, is to indicate that what we have is really worthless. We respond to a compliment with, "It's not really anything," or "Oh, thank you, but anyone could do it." Americans, who fear envy for some accomplishment, make sure to compliment others on their skills or hide or devalue their own accomplishment.[63]

***

Clearly, many other mechanisms are used to ward off envy. However the most effective, but most self-destructive, defense against envy and the "evil eye" is making sure there is nothing about you to be envied. Being fat is one way to do just that. *Being fat is a way to advertise, no one need envy my physical appearance.* Consequently, some people unconsciously become fat to protect themselves from the "evil eye" or the envy of another. To them, feeling unattractive is less painful than being envied.

Two

"Mirror, Mirror on The Wall"

Although everyone has felt envy, it is an emotion most people are very uncomfortable acknowledging. Envy feels mean, selfish, and hostile. Julie Harris says, "'Envy is a confining, enslaving emotion. When you are envious, you try to suppress it. Any emotion you suppress most of the time goes inward and gives you bile. Envy has a bitterness, a rancor, that makes you sick.'"[64]

> "Mirror, Mirror, on the wall,
> Who's the fairest one of all?"

These famous words from the Brothers Grimm's fairy tale, *Snow White*, are spoken by a person with intense envy. In the story Snow White's stepmother used a magic mirror to ask if she was the most beautiful woman in the world. One day the mirror replied:

> "Lady Queen, you are the most beautiful here
> But Snow White is a thousand times more beautiful than you."

The queen was outraged and green with envy. Her feelings of envy were so intense, she ordered a hunter to kill Snow White.

Envy, as depicted in the fairy tale, is an emotion that in its most intense form, is replete with the desire for the envied person to suffer or die.

It is no wonder some people go to extremes to avoid being the object of envy. To avoid the sting of envy, some people even do self destructive things, such as becoming obese. Carla, a thirty eight year old woman puts it this way. "Either I can be beautiful and hated and lonely. Or I can be fat, but loved and secure. Everyone knows people are envious of a winner."

In reality, envy literally can be deadly. Consider the murder conspiracy of the cheerleader's mother popularized in the movie, "The Positively True Adventures of the Alleged Texas Cheerleader-Murdering Mom."[65] This mother of a teenage girl was intensely envious of another girl, whom, she feared would surpass her daughter in a cheerleading competition. Her envy was so profound that she actually hired someone to murder the girl's mother.

***

A woman in Munich, while taking her friend's baby out for a walk, pushed the baby carriage into the river. The psychiatrist working on the case, indicated that the woman was suddenly overcome with envy of her friend's happiness, which her baby personified.[66]

***

In Victorville, California, newspapers printed a story headline reading "'Jealous of Woman's Wealth, Boy says in Iron-Rod Killing.'" On March 15, 1960 a seventeen year old boy killed his friend's mother, because he was envious of the family's wealth.[67]

***

In Georgia another seventeen year old boy shot his friend to death. The alleged motive was that he was envious his friend had been elected class president.[68]

***

The common metaphor "dressed to kill," reveals the envious person's fantasy to harm someone. When someone "dresses to kill," she reveals her wish to emotionally devastate through envy.

***

Helmut Schoeck, writing about the emotion of envy, states although envy is an inherent part of all human existence, it is one of the most disturbing and greatly concealed emotions.[69] Pathological envy comes from inner feelings of dissatisfaction. It may be that the envier not only wants to acquire something someone else has, but may want to be the only one to have it. The envier may want to be the only talented, famous, successful, beautiful, youthful, person in the whole world. Basically, that person wants to be the only one in the world who is really loved. This desire, if fulfilled, would safeguard the person from ever feeling unloved or unimportant.

The feeling of intense envy causes the envier great pain. Sometimes, the envy is so great that it pervades the individual's entire life. The envy makes the enjoyment of what she does have impossible, because the only thing that concerns her is what she does not have.

Being the object of another's envy is quite threatening to many people. All of us are somewhat uncomfortable with being envied, because of its intrinsic hostility and reflection of malevolence. Many people with good fortune are fearful of being disliked, punished or actually harmed because of another's envy.

Some people believe if they have nothing to envy, they will be protected from the potential envier's malice. When an individual *unconsciously* uses this type of defense against envy, she may feel protected. She is protected, however, at a great price. Becoming fat may protect her from being envied, but it does not protect her from the pain of feeling unattractive. Ironically, this same person may herself become very envious of those who are slim.

Three

A Voracious Hunger

What causes envy?

Towards our second birthday, our ability to distinguish between ourselves and others expands. At this stage we seek to acquire and possess things for ourselves. Hand-in-hand with these desires occur manifestations of envy. We begin to have intense feelings of rivalry with our parents, siblings and others, who have what we want, but do not have. At first the focus of acquisition is on our mothers. We become acutely aware of who has more attention and love from her. Later, our desire for acquisitions relate to other things as well. We assess who is bigger, who has greater capabilities, and who can control whom. We want it all, and we envy those who have what we do not.

The recognition of what we have and do not have, promotes the development of our self image and identity, but it also contributes to intense ambivalent feelings toward our rivals. At first, the feelings of hostile envy, admiration, and the desire to be more like our rival coexist. As with the resolution of ambivalence towards our mother, the intense ambivalence toward our rivals subsides only when our love and admiration for our rivals prevail over our hostile, envious, jealous and negative feelings.

***

Intense envy dominates when there is not enough loving, admiring and grateful feelings to counterbalance the angry, hostile and rivalrous feelings. When we are overly frustrated and unfulfilled during our early childhood stages, envy can take the form of a *voracious hunger* which needs to be denied. This hunger, which is unconscious and unknown, may lead to symptoms such as compulsive eating or the overwhelming fear of being taken over by this hunger and getting fat.

Four

"I Thought If I Became Pretty My Mother Would Die"

As unbelievable as it may seem, envy can even be experienced by a parent toward a child. Experiencing envy from a parent is a very confusing and frightening feeling for a child. Since we need our parents in order to feel secure and loved, feeling their hostility is truly threatening.

***

Sandra, a woman I treated, had a very envious mother. She was frequently the recipient of her mother's hostility. Understandably, this was truly confusing to her. She did not know what she had done to cause her mother's hatred. When she was young she elaborated a fantasy that her mother wanted to murder her. This was the only way she could comprehend her mother's animosity. In the style of Cinderella's wicked stepmother, Sandra's mother made her wear ugly, sometimes torn clothes. She never bought Sandra any foods she liked, in fact Sandra was made to eat different foods from the rest of the family. Her mother pushed her to succeed, so she could be the mother of a successful daughter. However, when she did succeed, her mother expressed hostility towards her.

***

Why would a parent feel hostile envy towards her own child? An envious person who feels dissatisfied with herself and her own life, can easily become an envious parent. The envy may be evoked because, as in the tale of Snow White, the child has youth, beauty and a whole life ahead of her, while the mother or father's life is heading towards middle age and decreased opportunities. The parent can be envious because the envied child reminds him or her of an envied sibling. A parent, who was orphaned, can envy a child for merely having the parents he or she did not have. A child who has a particular attribute, such as talent, intelligence, or beauty may evoke envy in a parent who coveted those attributes. Mothers or fathers may envy a child for being parented in the way he or she longed to be. A child can be envied for having opportunities in a world which were not available to the parent. In contemporary society, freedom to have choices regarding marriage, premarital sex, independence, and career, are freedoms many parents, especially mothers, did not have. Mothers and fathers may be envious of the child's ability to focus completely on his or her own happiness, with little regard for responsibilities to a family.

***

An obese woman speaks about hating being fat, but being afraid of the alternative. She says, "When I was twelve, my mother said to me, 'My turn is over it's your turn now.' I thought if I became pretty my mother would die, so I made a decision not to enter the competition."[70] Being envied by a parent can be terrifying. This woman made a decision to be fat rather than provoke her mother's envy.

***

"I realized I was keeping myself fat so I wouldn't have more than she did. I acknowledged it to myself, but instead of letting go of it, I held onto it to protect me. By being fat I was showing my mother I was not to be envied. I was her clone, not a threatening rival."[71] These are the thoughts of Renee Taylor, the coauthor with her husband, Joe Bologna, of the play "Lovers and Other Strangers." Actually Renee Taylor started out studying to be an actress, her mother's life-long, but failed, ambition. To avoid her mother's envy, Ms. Taylor avoided acting for some time and pursued writing instead. Presently, Ms. Taylor is fulfilling both her dreams; she acts and writes.

Helen

Helen was a thirty-five year old woman who was 40 pounds overweight. Objectively, she was a charming, attractive and successful woman, however she did not perceive of herself in that way. She came in to see me because she was depressed. She had just been promoted and was earning more money than she ever believed she could. Consequently, she did not understand why she was so depressed. Prior to this promotion, she believed if she could enjoy a career position which evoked admiration, she would feel happy. But now, even after assuming this prestigious position, she was not happy.

In our work together Helen appeared to be in a great deal of pain. She would complain about her husband, saying he only cared about building a financial empire. However, it seemed to me, from other things she said, her husband cared about her a great deal. He would often spend time supporting, encouraging and listening to her. Several times a week, he would arrange his law practice so he could meet her for lunch. On special occasions he would surprise her with lovely gifts. Despite this, she said he really did not love her.

Helen expressed a great deal of disappointment in other areas of her life as well. She related that her twelve year old daughter was self-centered and selfish. Her daughter was a straight A student, but Helen insisted grades were all she cared about. Again, despite her complaints about her daughter, it appeared that she, her daughter and her husband got along relatively well.

Interactions with friends brought about similar complaints. She did not believe anyone really cared about her. She continually compared herself, unfavorably, to her friends and colleagues and was intensely rivalrous towards them. Inevitably, she found herself coming up short in every arena of her life.

Through our work we discovered the reason for her distress. No matter how well she did in her career or how good she felt with her family, she was not able to enjoy pleasure. She was terrified that if anyone knew how fortunate she was, they would be extremely envious of her, withdraw their love, or worse, hurt her in some way. Because of this, she felt impelled to hide her happiness from others and even herself.

Consequently, when her husband bought her presents, as a token of his love, she would never wear the gifts openly when she was with friends. When friends or colleagues complained about their husband's lack of attention or success, she would complain that her husband was always too busy for her. The days she would meet her husband for lunch, she would tell co-workers that she had some errands to do. She feared evoking their envy if she acknowledged with whom she had a lunch date.

Actually, her daughter was everything she always dreamed of in a daughter. She was smart and personable and very popular. Since Helen never felt popular as a child, she longed to have a daughter who was popular and everybody's favorite. But Helen feared that others would envy and dislike her, if they knew of her joy.

Helen did other things to deemphasize herself. She dressed in a dowdy manner wearing dull, drab colors and clothes that were devoid of style. Her hairstyle took away from, rather than enhanced, her pretty face. She accentuated her weight by wearing clothes that brought attention to it. She devalued her promotion, often saying, "It and a token would get her on the subway." Her home, though always clean and neat, was described as "nothing special to look at."

It was especially difficult for her to acknowledge all this to me. She feared if I knew how lucky she was and how good things were, I would be overwhelmingly envious of her and hurt her too.

Helen had good reason for her fear of other's envy. It was a fear founded on real experience. Her mother was very envious of Helen. Helen experienced hostility and envy from her mother from the time she entered her teens. For many years, Helen did not identify it as envy. She did not think it was possible for a parent to envy a child. She asked, "Aren't parents supposed to love their child?" But eventually she realized envy was exactly what it was.

Each time Helen enjoyed some success or happiness, her mother responded with indifference or anger. The anger was usually focused indirectly. But eventually, Helen got the point. For instance, when Helen did well in school, her mother mockingly replied, "That's fine, but you'd do better directing your attention towards cleaning your room." When Helen was excited about a date, her mother would ridicule and devalue the boy.

Helen noticed that any time she shared happiness with her mother, her mother would verbally attack her. The only thing that would bring a supportive response from her mother was when she was ill or unhappy. So unconsciously, in response, Helen frequently felt ill and unhappy. This continued throughout her teenage years into adulthood. Whenever she spoke to her mother, rather than emphasizing all the good things that were happening, she focused on how tired or ill she felt and how difficult things were for her. When she did that, her mother was supportive.

Her mother, she realized, was a very unhappy, frightened, unfulfilled woman, who was very envious of her own daughter. She responded, as many do who still need their mother's love and approval; she sacrificed her own happiness for her mother's love.

Through therapy Helen was able to become aware of what she was unconsciously doing. In time, she was able to enjoy her good fortune and pursue her desires including maintaining a weight with which she was happy.

Five

I'm Just an Unattractive, Unassuming Fat Individual

My cellulite is prominent
My thighs clap, can't you see?
My flab swings with a rhythm
No need to envy me!

— Diane Fero

The person who is the recipient of envy feels as if she is the object of hatred and malice. She experiences the hostility of the envier and feels utterly helpless to do anything about this ostensibly undeserved attack. The person who is envied often feels hurt, confused and threatened. If she tries to work things out between herself and her assaulter, she will be doomed to failure. For the very existence of the envied is the problem for the envier. The envier wants to hurt, humiliate and damage the envied one. "The envied one often feels stunned at this revelation that his or her being is the problem to the envier, and feels even more helpless to do anything as a result. For what is there to do? Like a victim of racial or sexual prejudice, the envied feels his essential self is under attack, not some fault or virtue that is changeable or detachable from one's central identity. Instead, one's very hold on life, one's connection to the good, is the problem."[72]

"The envied grow increasingly desperate, for nothing succeeds in warding off envy. If they renounce any hope of being seen and accepted as themselves, they are accused of being cold and aloof. If they try to share their good, they are attacked for showing off or being patronizing. If they try to defend by explaining, they are not listened to, for explanations, will not fill up an empty envier. Even if some of the melodrama is lacking, they are in the position of hostages being held by terrorists."[73]

***

Oprah Winfrey, who is loved and admired by many, was quoted: "Once I drop the weight which I'm going to, so ya'll get ready and envy me, just envy me one of the reasons I think I've held onto it is because, first of all, it gives people something to feel sorry for you about 'cause you have everything else, but you don't have great thighs, you see. So you use that so that they can't envy you because they have something you don't have."[74]

***

It is somewhat understandable then, that some envied individuals, who believe they are totally helpless against this onslaught of envy, think and act as if it would be better not to have so much or be so fortunate.

***

Some people who are overweight are so, because being overweight offers them a protection against envy. Being fat conveys to the potential envier, "Look I have nothing that you want. There is no need to hate me. I'm just an unattractive, unassuming fat individual." It is certain that anyone who needs to resort to such drastic measures to defend against envy, has had profoundly painful experiences of being envied. Becoming fat for that reason is not only a shield against envy, it is a reaction to having already felt the assault and hurt of an envier.

***

A woman recalls, "At the college dorm, girls envied me for being more attractive and thinner than they were. Of course, if you've been a second-class citizen, you're bound to envy. They gossiped about me. I was deeply hurt, devastated. Now, I am cautious not to 'look too good' and often won't do things I want to do, like acting on a stage, because I am fearful of arousing envy in other women."[75]

***

Talking about discovering her mother dead after a heart attack, the actress Renee Taylor said, "At least she died thinking I was on my way to being a big star. Or did that idea kill her—That it was to be me and not her . . . . I judged myself guilty on so many counts, most of all that I had a happier marriage than she did. I had all these reasons to get fat again . . . ."[76]

Ilene

Ilene is a forty year old attractive, overweight, successful lawyer. Being successful in her career and having many close friends are things she greatly values. However what is most important to her, but continually eludes her, is her desire to be happy in a love relationship. Ilene avoids relationships with men because she is ashamed of her body. She is certain that any man she would be interested in would find her body repugnant.

Since she was a teenager, Ilene had difficulty losing weight. Before that, her weight was not a problem. When she was about sixteen years old, she began to gain weight very quickly. Her mother responded to her distress about her weight gain in a casual way, telling Ilene not to worry about it. When she succeeded in dieting and lost some weight, her mother would be very critical and rejecting of her.

Her mother always spoke about herself as someone whom the guys chased after. She said she was always considered the prettiest girl in her school. Her mother had entered and won several beauty contests. And even now people commented about how young she looked. Moreover, her mother would say that people thought Ilene was her sister; she looked so young, they could not believe she was a mother.

When Ilene was a child, the relationship she had with her mother was a good one. Her mother would be approving when Ilene got good grades, had many friends and partook in many extracurricular activities. She would fuss over Ilene's appearance, as much as she did her own.

However, that all changed when Ilene became interested in boys. Ilene experienced her mother as continually angry with her. It seemed to Ilene that her mother's anger was directed at her being popular with boys. Being pretty and desirable to men was always her mother's claim to fame.

When Ilene became interested in boys, her mother stopped taking an interest in her appearance. In fact she seemed to express annoyance whenever a boy called Ilene. When male friends did come to visit Ilene, her mother would criticize Ilene in their company and vie for the boy's attention herself.

When she was around sixteen, Ilene began to lose interest in boys and started to gain weight. By age seventeen she was thirty pounds overweight. Ilene's weight gain was an unconscious defense against her mother's envy. Because Ilene still needed her mother's love and approval, she protected herself by gaining weight to avert her mother's envy. As Ilene became heavy, her mother became more loving. She even appeared to help Ilene with diets and meal plans. However, as soon as Ilene would begin to show any significant weight loss, her mother would become critical of one thing or another.

Through analysis Ilene became aware of why she resisted losing weight and having a relationship with a man. She was able to see how she responded to her mother's tacit threat. Fortunately, Ilene found a healthier way to deal with her mother's envy, lost the weight she wanted to and began to date men again.

Six

Being Beautiful and Tolerating Envy

A voiding being envied and therefore hated, is one powerful reason some people, unconsciously, wish to be fat. Everyone finds it painful to tolerate another's hatred. However, remaining fat to avoid hatred always fails. Because being fat ultimately results in self hatred.

People who are so fearful of envy they would consciously or unconsciously become fat to avoid it, have usually suffered greatly from envy when they were young. They may have experienced a loss of love, due to envy, which was very much needed during that time in their life. For example, being the object of envy from a parent, whose love is essential for our feeling of well being, would be devastating to most people. Experiencing hateful feelings from one's own parent usually is so painful and frightening, it often results in the child doing whatever possible to regain the love of the parent, including getting fat. Later on in life, the feeling of danger associated with looking well or being otherwise successful, is generalized to all. The person believes that no one, or no one whose love is important, will love her if she looks too pretty or is too successful.

***

If you have become aware that fear of envy is contributing to your being overweight, there are several important things you must recognize. First of all, everyone has feelings of envy. These are very uncomfortable feelings so some people disavow them. But we all feel envy. And despite all the envy around us, we can observe many people who are slim, well functioning, successful and relatively happy. We can acknowledge, although people who are successful and happy are being envied, they seem to be able to tolerate it and survive it. In fact, although people who are successful are often envied, they are also admired, frequently by the same people who envy them. That is because there are different degrees of envy. Most people's envy is not intense enough to disallow other more positive feelings. Most people's envy does not result in the abandonment of the envied person.

***

Once again, if you are tempted to eat something not in accordance with your diet use the <u>10 minute</u> exercise previously outlined. During this time remind yourself how important being thin is to you. Focus on your knowledge of what your overeating is actually about. Think about this knowledge and awareness when you think about fearing others' envy if you become slim. Identify specifically which persons' envy you fear. Assess how threatening their envy actually would be if it was evoked. Might they be envious and not let it interfere with your relationship? Would they be envious and distance themselves from you slightly for a short period of time? Think about what you can do to tolerate that kind of envy. You might, for example, reassure yourself that this feeling is normal and will probably be short lived. You could remind yourself of all the people who would be happy about your success, and deemphasize this one particular person's envy. Perhaps you could even talk to the envious person and let her (him) know you miss the closeness you have shared in the past and greatly value the relationship. Sometimes, envious people abandon others, whom they believe have surpassed them, for fear they will be abandoned by them.

Is there someone in your life whom you believe actually would abandon you and hate you completely, if you were thin? This kind of envy is rare, but does exist. Believing you truly will be hated by someone whose love is very important to you, presents a real problem. You need to chose between being what you want to be, slim in this case, or having the love of someone you value. That is a difficult choice. However, when you think about it in those terms, you may become aware of angry feelings regarding your need to sacrifice your self esteem and health, for the love of someone who does not share your wishes for success and happiness. Perhaps, with that in mind, you will be able to have the courage to risk the envy and even loss of love of this person, in order to gain your own self love and self respect.

As I said before, it is my experience that most people who risk abandonment to achieve their own goals, rarely actually experience the permanent abandonment they feared. Sometimes it occurs temporarily.

But if the person continues pursuing her goals, usually the abandoning person adapts and resumes the relationship in a different but healthier way. Finally, being aware of your fears and consciously struggling and ultimately succeeding in coming to terms with them, frequently brings about a feeling of power and the ability to deal with any harsh envy which does emerge.

***

Remember all the things you thought about your fear of being envied. Develop creative ideas to deal with envy if it does emerge. Picture yourself thin, having greater self esteem and sufficient self love to tolerate any envy or loss. Call a friend who is supportive of your quest for a beautiful you. Think of all the people who will be happy for you when you achieve your goal.

Remember to praise and reward yourself for any success you realized, diverting yourself from eating foods you wished to avoid. You did a great job and should feel proud of yourself!

Part Six

Failing To Eat Or Eating To Fail — Masochism

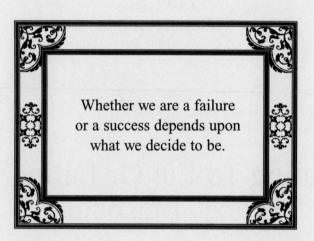

Whether we are a failure
or a success depends upon
what we decide to be.

One

Failing to Eat or Eating to Fail Masochism

Being fat and thinking one's body is the object of ridicule or revulsion, may be an expression of the unconscious desire for pain or humiliation.

Marcia Millman discusses how some members of NAAFA (National Association to Aid Fat Americans) sought men's rejection as if it were a motivating force in their lives. She ascribed this to family dynamics in the backgrounds of these women. These women had childhoods fraught with rejecting attitudes from their fathers. As adults they eroticized the rejection by falling in love with men who would reject them. With the unconscious desire to repeat the relationship with their father, they choose men who would inevitably withhold love from them and humiliate them. She describes one woman whose boyfriend insisted she watch him flirt with other women. And she did. These women, described as fulfilling masochistic needs, did everything they could to please. Some of them acknowledged feeling they deserved to be abused because of guilt regarding sexuality. Abusive treatment by men was consistent with the self contempt and shame they felt about themselves.[77]

***

Consider the tale of a man who signs a contract with a woman named Wanda.

"He signs a contract with Wanda renouncing his identity completely; agreeing to submit totally to her will, to thoroughly follow her orders and be her 'slave groveling in the dust.' He agrees to allow her to 'exercise the greatest cruelty' and to bear mutilation without complaint. The contract further specifies, 'You shall work for me like a slave and although I may wallow in luxury whilst leaving you in privation and treading you underfoot, you shall kiss the foot that tramples you without a murmur.—

I have the power and right to torture you to death by the most horrible methods imaginable.'"

As soon as he signed the contract he "knelt down before her in sweet rapture and laid my head on her breast.— She began to whip me again.

"— The warm blood began to run but she laughed and continued to whip me.

"— I approached my cruel, mocking beauty who seemed more seductive than ever before."[78]

This was how Sacher-Masoch, the author of *Venus In Furs*,[79] described his passion for a woman who treated him with extreme cruelty and coldness. He displaced his love for the cruel and cold goddess statue of Venus onto a woman Wanda, whom he seduced into being his cruel and sadistic beloved.

***

The term masochism, coined by Richard von Krafft-Ebing, describes a syndrome that Leopold von Sacher-Masoch wrote about in the nineteenth century. His stories, based on his own feelings, reflected men who wished to suffer, especially sexually, by a woman's hand. Today the term masochism is not reserved for men who wish painful sexual experiences. More broadly speaking, a masochistic person is characterized as someone who brings about his or her own painful existence. This pain may be brought about by the provocation or toleration of abuse, failing, humiliation, ridicule, self depreciation and so on. The masochist seems to contradict the principle that the central motivating force in all human behavior is the achievement of pleasure, or at least the avoidance of displeasure. Because of that, we must assume the actual goal of masochism is other than suffering. The suffering must be viewed as a means to another end. Why suffering is used to bring about desired aims is a complex question with complex answers.

Basically, the masochist suffers. In fact, the masochist unconsciously arranges for and desires to suffer. Many theories have evolved to explain masochism, which may function in different ways for particular people.

The masochistic individuals that Jack and Kerry Kelly Novick[80] studied had mothers who were unable to respond with pleasure to their child, due to their own depression. One of their patients described their home as having an odor of unhappiness. These people continued suffering as adults, as suffering was familiar and therefore, in some way, comforting. For them, feeling happy was tantamount to feeling alone, and too separate from their family.

If an infant frequently is unable to elicit his mother's response when he cries and calls to be rescued, he consequently experiences a sense of rage, despair and hopelessness. Regarding this kind of early experience, the seeking out of pain can be viewed as a means of feeling alive, of existing. Feeling pain allows the person to affirm his existence in the way his parents did not. To this person, it is better to feel pain than nothing.

Toddlers normally become assertive, defiant, and seek to be independent of their mothers. This is the way all of us begin to experience our identity, who we are, vis-a-vis the rest of the world. The stage of the "terrible twos" is reflective of this state of being. If a toddler's parents do not respond appropriately to this normal ambivalence, aggression and search for autonomy, the toddler's aggression may intensify. If that aggression is met by mother's anger, the child will feel guilty and responsible for his mother's pain. This may set the stage for the masochistic individual who uses his ability to evoke rage in his mother as testimony of his magical omnipotent powers. Since his mother, who denies him independence, seems to own his body, hurting himself is tantamount to hurting his mother. This feeling is reflected in the thought, "I'll hurt myself and you'll be sorry." The feeling of total helplessness is thereby eliminated through omnipotent fantasies of control and destructiveness.

In some cases, the masochist unconsciously sacrifices his own independence and competence, creating a devalued sense of himself, as a way of holding on to the wished for all powerful mother of childhood, on whom he can depend. The masochistic self-debasement serves the function of providing the fantasy of being intimately connected to or merged with a superior, powerful person. When this person experiences himself as competent and adequate, he suffers the loss of feeling connected to that all powerful parent figure. Consequently, he arranges to feel like a failure to perpetuate the fantasy that a powerful person is taking care of him.

For others, masochism serves as punishment for unconscious prohibited wishes stemming from the oedipal phase of childhood development. In this case the individual seeks pain as punishment for forbidden incestuous wishes and protection from the intense guilt related to those wishes. Since he is experiencing a painful punishment, manifested in whichever way he arranges to suffer, his guilt is assuaged.

Suffering expiates guilt for conscious or unconscious aggressive and sadistic wishes as well. The aggression, which is conscious or unconscious, is regarded as dangerous and indicative of one's badness. Suffering allays the guilt for the forbidden impulses. The punishment of suffering is sought also to assist in curbing one's aggressiveness.

Suffering and experiencing pain may be a way a person connects with another. This situation occurs when a child gets more attention from his parents when he is in pain than when he is happy. The person associates pain with love and connectedness. As an adult, the person displaces the feelings he had with his parent on to other significant people in his life and continues to relate to others through suffering. Some parents may subtly or otherwise put pressure on a child to be intimate through suffering. When a child, even a grown-up child, talks about happy things occurring, that parent may be indifferent or critical. But when that child conveys how unhappy or distressed he or she is, that parent becomes very attentive, loving and helpful. Many children respond to their parent's desperate need to be needed by suffering.

Identification is another way a person may connect with another through suffering. For example, a child whose parent suffered from chronic depression may feel intimately connected to this parent, by also suffering. The child becomes a person whose lot in life is to suffer. Suffering, on some level, helps him feel connected to, and often approved of by his suffering parent. It is as if the child is saying to the parent we are the same, different from the others, and that makes us happy even though it is through misery.

Masochistically exhibited suffering can be used as a way of disarming a potential attacker. By doing more damage to oneself than another would do, another's guilt and indulgence is evoked. The suffering thereby serves as a way to thwart off an anticipated attack. It is common reaction for most of us to "make nice" to someone who is suffering. "I put myself down before someone else does," and "If I put myself down others will reassure me and tell me I'm okay," are typical thoughts of people who suffer to appease someone they believe will attack them. The fantasy or belief that others will put them down is usually constant. And the concomitant suffering and belief in their inadequacy is authentic. Often the knowledge that they are keeping themselves feeling inadequate to allay an attack is unconscious.

Being painfully inferior can function as a way to evoke another's help. The show of suffering and need can be used to coerce another to feel guilty and consequently, to give of himself to the sufferer. The exhibition of suffering can express sadistic wishes toward another by inducing the helper to feel impotent. No matter how the other tries to help the masochist feel better, he fails. The dance goes like this: "Help me please, I am suffering. I don't know what to do." The helper responds, "Don't worry I'll show you how to do it, it's easy." The sufferer responds, "Help me please, I am suffering. I don't know what to do." Anyone who's played the role of the helper experiences the intended frustration, guilt and feeling of impotence.

A significant factor of masochism is the dramatization of the misery before a real or imagined audience. The response the masochist desires varies. He may wish to evoke expressions of concern or sympathy, or he may seek to punish the audience through the evocation of guilt or remorse. What remains constant is that the masochist is not being ignored; his suffering has an impact on the audience.

Masochism can manifest itself in many ways. The masochist can be conscious of the fact he enjoys pain and suffering, or more likely, the desire to suffer is unconscious. The suffering experienced by the masochist can take various forms. A masochist may bring about suffering by putting pressure on others to hurt him emotionally or physically. Many of us have experienced this pressure to treat another badly. We respond to someone in a cruel way and then we feel guilty. What we do not realize is, we are not mean people; we are being induced to behave this way.

Unconsciously arranging to fail at everything one does is another manifestation of a masochist's need to suffer. The sufferer may report he expends much effort trying to succeed at various things. The listener feels sorry and at times guilty or responsible. However, closer observation reveals the sufferer is orchestrating his own defeat.

Maxine

Maxine was a forty-five year old attractive, quite overweight, married social worker. Her husband was a fifty-one year old successful business executive, who was extremely self centered and abusive. Maxine's relationship with him could have been described as sado-masochistic. She responded to her husband's cruel ridicule of her cooking, intelligence, and fat appearance by crying, apologizing and promising to do better. Each week she turned her paycheck over to her husband, who decided where their joint monies would be spent. Although his spending decisions inevitably focused on his sporting equipment and hobbies, she insisted she was pleased when he was happy and therefore did not resent him. Her suffering was revealed by her sad expression, which her husband condemned, and her tales of woe which she shared with her mother and friends.

Maxine began treatment due to depression, although she was vague about the nature of her distress. She was promoted at her job at a social service agency; nevertheless she believed her employers did not like her. She thought they believed she was not bright enough and not "with it," meaning naive. Her self esteem was quite poor; she believed she was not attractive enough, thin enough, smart enough, witty enough, lovable enough and so on. Because of these things, she was certain that inevitably she would be abandoned by all.

Her marriage was terrible. Her husband would invariably talk down to her and treat her like hired help. He expected her to be available to him at a moments notice. He might call her fifteen minutes before he was coming home with colleagues and expect her to prepare an impressive dinner. Frequently though, he did not come home at all for dinner. And more often than not, did not call. "If I'm not here you should know I'm not coming home," he'd say. She hid her feelings whenever she ever felt angry with him. In fact she would feel guilty for feeling angry, believing if she were a good and understanding wife she would not feel angry.

Maxine conveyed to me over and over again how painful her life was. Although she rarely complained about how she was being treated, her anguish was consistently revealed through her anecdotes. Analysis of Maxine was difficult, as even in the therapy situation she needed to suffer.

She thoroughly shared every aspect of her painful life. On the other hand, when something particularly good occurred for her, she withheld it from me. I would find out about it when she inadvertently mentioned it, perhaps months after the event, while telling me about something else she was suffering about. Additionally, when something positive occurred in her life, her suffering would intensify.

Ultimately, we learned that Maxine believed she deserved to suffer because she was guilty of something terrible. She remembered, as a child, wishing that her mother would die so she could be her father's wife. Suffering functioned as a punishment, as well as a protection from God's even harsher punishment. God would not punish her, she believed, if she suffered. Suffering also provided her with a way to connect with and receive approval from an otherwise distant and critical mother.

Maxine's choice of husband was not bad luck or her misfortune. Unconsciously she chose him for several reasons. One was that he reminded her of her father in both appearance and personality, her father was tall and trim and had a moustache just like her husband. In addition, her father, like her husband, was a successful take charge type of person. Her father treated her mother as poorly as Maxine's husband treated her. Choosing this man to marry was unconsciously and symbolically marrying her father. Also, it was a punishment for that wish, as she was victimized and bullied by this man. It was a way to placate her mother, demonstrating to her that she was not any happier and therefore did not triumph over her. Although she dared not deny her husband sex, she never enjoyed intercourse, or had an orgasm. This served as another way to punish herself for "forbidden" wishes, while simultaneously enacting those same wishes. Maxine had arranged her life to be a continuous punishment for wishing and enacting forbidden sexual desires.

Carol

Carol was an attractive thirty-five year old, overweight, married woman when she came to see me due to a lifetime of feeling depressed. She finally sought help when she was so depressed, it was difficult for her to get out of bed in the morning to go to work. She described herself as continually feeling inadequate, so much so, she believed she would be imminently fired from her job as a secretary, due to her inferior work. She frequently cried about this to her husband Gene, a thirty five year old accountant, who, she stated, was not always sympathetic. Carol's wished her husband would commiserate with her about her difficult job, and suggest she quit and stay home.

Carol's feelings of inadequacy had no bounds. She suffered incessantly, as she thought about her failure to make good friends, to look well and to finish college. Carol bemoaned looking like a slob, "fat, with ugly clothes." She believed she could not do anything about her weight because she was "weak willed," and she could not do anything about her clothes because her husband would resent her spending money on new clothes. When asked about why she could not spend the money she earned herself on clothes which would make her feel better, she indicated she was afraid her husband would get angry and leave her.

From all impressions given, there appeared to be no basis for her fear her employer, friends and husband would soon find her lacking. Her husband did not suggest he wished to leave her at any time during their fifteen year marriage. She worked for the same law firm for four years with ostensibly no serious complaint about her work. Her friendships were few, but they did not appear to be rejecting.

Yet her depression and suffering about her inadequacy and impending abandonment was ceaseless. No matter what insight and understanding she gained in therapy, her suffering continued.

We ultimately discovered the reason for Carol's suffering. Carol grew up with a critical, opinionated, domineering and rejecting mother who behaved hatefully towards Carol. Seemingly, the only way Carol was able to gain any positive response from her mother was when she was needy and dependent on her. In therapy, Carol talked about her mother as someone whom she hated and had little respect for. However, Carol had other unconscious feelings which were revealed in fantasies and dreams. Carol wished to be intimately connected to her all powerful mother, and have her take complete care and control of her. In her fantasies and dreams Carol was a little helpless child, completely dependent on this powerful, sometimes sadistic woman.

From this history we were able to understand Carol's present suffering. Carol transferred the relationship she had with her mother onto all her other relationships. She related to others, including her therapist, as if their positive response would be forthcoming only if she suffered and was dependent. And so suffer she did. She suffered and experienced herself as completely inadequate and at the mercy of everyone she loved. She suffered to maintain her fantasy she was connected to her powerful mother who would protect her and take care of her. Feeling debased, low, and inadequate was necessary for her to preserve that fantasy. Although she seemed to suffer endlessly, on some level she felt comforted by the belief that some powerful person, her husband, her therapist or her mother, was taking care of her.

Carol married a man she regarded as competent and powerful who was very controlling and therefore often did take care of her, which made her feel safe and nurtured. Although she complained her husband was controlling her and not allowing her to feel equal and adequate, she dared not be, for doing so would result in the loss of her fantasy that she was being taken care of. Carol convinced herself she had no say about what occurred in her marriage or even what clothes she bought for herself, because unconsciously, she wished to hold on to the fantasy that she was with her strong, critical, rejecting and opinionated mother/husband who was taking care of her. Carol related to her husband and the rest of the world, as an inadequate needy little girl. She debased herself in many ways, including being fat and being unable to "get herself together," in order to maintain this fantasy.

Ultimately, recognizing the price she was paying to maintain this fantasy, Carol was able to begin to take greater control over her life. In time, she worked out a different, more equal, relationship with her husband. Carol

went back to college and attained a degree. She pursued a higher level
career and she eventually lost sufficient weight for her to feel attractive.

Freedom from Suffering

Realizing being overweight may be a manifestation of masochism is painful in itself. Losing weight which is connected to the desire for pain and suffering is difficult, if not impossible, without resolving the masochism itself. For remember, the point of masochism is to suffer. To attain the goal of a better body image and a happier self is in contradiction to the needs of a masochist.

Recognizing that masochistic tendencies may be influencing your life is a good first step. Think about and try to identify what function suffering may be serving for you. Think about how else that need may be fulfilled, other than through masochistic behavior.

Masochism, at times, is related to the desire to debase oneself to unconsciously hold onto the all powerful parent of infancy or childhood. This need is so great that the suffering person will keep herself (or himself) devalued to maintain this fantasy. If this person were to experience herself (or himself) as a competent and adequate person, a feeling of loss of the powerful symbolic parent would ensue. To this person, the loss feels so devastating, that unconsciously he or she would prefer to feel inadequate and devalued, than to suffer that loss. Consider whether you wish to continue to experience yourself as inadequate and inferior, merely to maintain a fantasy of being connected with someone powerful. To fulfill your conscious wish to be thin, you must be determined to make feeling small and inadequate in relationship to a powerful symbolic parent, completely unacceptable. If you discover yourself negating your competency, recognize these thoughts as simply echoing your masochistic tendencies. Instead of devaluing and demeaning what you do, regard what you do in more realistic terms.

The dynamics of some people's masochism is to feel pain to assuage the guilt related to oedipal wishes. Many people, unconsciously, keep themselves fat to avoid being tempted to have sex with "the wrong, prohibited person." If you begin to develop awareness of guilt feelings related to those issues, it is essential that you recognize that oedipal wishes are normal, not bad or wrong. Recognize you are causing yourself to feel unattractive in order to punish yourself for thoughts and feelings which are normal and typical of every child's development. Every little girl and every little boy wanted to marry their father or mother and get rid of their competing parent. Probably all of us, as children, were seductive toward one parent and had fantasies that parent loved us and desired us the most. That is normal. There is no need to be punished for *normal* childhood fantasies.

It is important to recognize that the person to whom you are attracted, who may resemble your parent, is *not your parent*. To be with that person sexually, is not committing incest. Your sexual and aggressive desires and fantasies are not *bad or wrong*; therefore, there is no need for you to suffer and be punished.

Gaining attention through suffering is another dynamic of masochism. Think about it. Do you wish to continue to gain attention by suffering? Think about why you may have needed to suffer to get attention. Contemplate other, healthier ways, you can get the attention you need. Perhaps suffering is the only way you can get attention from a particular person. Maybe that is how you always maintained intimacy with this person. To relate in a different manner may disrupt the feeling of intimacy between you and this other person. However, think about whether experiencing yourself as a suffering victim, is worth the intimacy gained. Is it possible to enjoy a relationship with this person, devoid of suffering, even if it is not as intimate as before? Think about whether you arrange all your relationships in such a way as to obtain attention through suffering. Contemplate whether you wish to continue to spend your life as a victim. Recognize that you are in control of changing that wish.

***

While you do the 10 minute exercise to postpone your urge to overeat think about why you want to eat at this time. Remind yourself of your wish to be thin. Decide if you want suffering to continue to be a fundamental part of your life. If you have forestalled your aim to binge, recognize this as a great achievement. Not only did you thwart your desire to undermine your goal of becoming thin, but you took the first step in doing something contrary to suffering and being a victim. Do not suffer and devalue what you did. It was wonderful! Recognize it can feel good to succeed. You can get just as much love and attention succeeding as failing. It is up to you. If the relationships you are presently in provide love and attention only when you fail, develop new ones. This is your life. You only have one; enjoy it. Do not forget to praise and reward yourself for any success you achieve in defeating your urge to overeat. You did a great job and you deserve it!

***

Masochism is a very complex problem and difficult to resolve by oneself. For some people suffering is the only way they feel alive. If you believe this force is significantly influencing your life, it may be helpful to seek out some professional help.

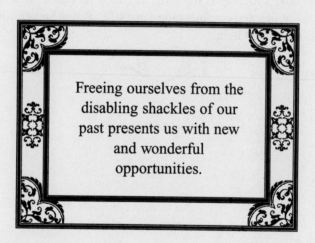

Freeing ourselves from the
disabling shackles of our
past presents us with new
and wonderful
opportunities.

Part Seven

Those Eating-My-Heart-Out Blues

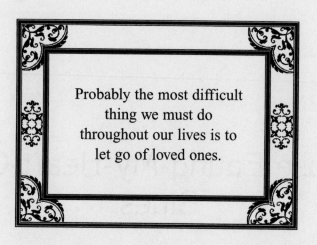

Probably the most difficult
thing we must do
throughout our lives is to
let go of loved ones.

One

Those Eating-My-Heart-Out Blues

The time that I am most susceptible to overeating is when something very disappointing or bad happens and I am feeling blue. Not everyone responds to distressing things by overeating as I do. In fact, not all overeaters turn to food when they feel down. It is a family joke that if someone we love becomes seriously ill or dies, my sister, who also is an overeater, loses weight and I gain weight. When my sister feels depressed her appetite shuts down. When I feel depressed I eat non-stop. Of course, since I am very conscious and motivated to remain slender, I do not allow this non-stop eating to go on for too long. I work hard to resolve my distress so I can feel better emotionally and I resume my diet and exercise regime.

***

It is quite common for overeaters to eat when they feel depressed. In fact a common reason for gaining a great deal of weight, is depression. The depression may be a chronic long lived, low level depression or it may be an acute depression, related to an event such as the loss of a loved one, a divorce or loss of a job.

When discussing depression, we are usually referring to a wide range of feelings which stem anywhere from our feeling a little down in the dumps, to being so depressed we want to die.

***

A clinical depression, that is, a psychiatrically defined depression, is characterized as a mood or feeling which reflects sadness, hopelessness, helplessness, guilt and self-critical thoughts. The manifestations of a clinical depression are, fatigue, insomnia, or a greater need for sleep, lack of appetite or overeating, diminished sexual drive and difficulty thinking and concentrating. A clinically depressed person exhibits a diminished interest in outside activities and an increased concern with oneself. A common feature of most depression is lowered self-esteem or feelings of worthlessness.

A person who suffers from a clinical depression has an illness which requires professional treatment, because it is often long lasting and debilitating. Depressive illness is different from a depressed or lowered mood, which often remits spontaneously or with resolution of the event or issue which precipitated it.

***

Be it just a state of the blues or a clinical depression, many people who feel depressed respond to those painful feelings by overeating.

"I'm depressed, so I'm stuffing my face." " I feel like shit, so I'm bingeing now." "I deserve to eat with abandon whatever I want, because I feel so bad." "I'm gorging myself because I'm depressed that I'm so fat." "I'll devour whatever I want. My outside might as well look as disgusting as my insides." "I'm so depressed the only thing I want to do is eat." These are all familiar refrains from overeaters who are depressed.

***

A depressed person feels the world is unable to offer him anything that will satisfy him. He feels both hungry and empty, yet certain there is nothing that could fill him. Therefore, there is no hope for gratification or remedy.

***

Ralph Greenson,[81] a noted psychoanalyst referred to the depressed person's sense of a bereft self. This person believes the world is filled with pleasures he is unable to partake in. Consequently he feels empty and hungry, like a "hungry motherless child."

***

Karl Abraham, a noted psychoanalyst writing in the early 1900s, stated, in regard to depression, the focus on the mouth and eating had two functions: to prevent an episode of depression and to remove it once it had occurred. He reported numerous observations of cravings, fantasies and symptoms that centered around the mouth in depressed patients. Fantasies of suckling and of biting the breasts or other parts of the loved one, were also common among these patients. Abraham, describing the soothing effect and function of eating to depressed people remembered a depressed male patient who, while putting a cup of milk to his mouth, said it felt like warm and soft and sweet combined.[82]

Abraham further postulated the melancholically depressed person regresses, unconsciously, to the oral phase of development and thereby wishes to incorporate, swallow and ingest the person he loves. He said that this wish is colored by hostility, however, so a desire to devour and to demolish this person simultaneously exists. He believed guilt associated with the hostile cannibalistic wishes accounted for the melancholic's refusal to eat.

***

A depressed patient stated, "I'm nothing, and nowhere. I feel empty and constantly hungry, but I don't know what for."

***

"My depression is intensified when I think of my depressing roll of fat that must be dieted off." So laments another depressed person.

***

George Gero, a psychoanalyst writing in the 1930s, discussed the ravenous hunger of many of his depressed patients. He believed that the person who tends to be depressed is primarily oral and longing for the love and warmth of his mother's protecting body.[83]

***

Sandor Rado, a psychoanalyst writing in the 1920s, equated fear of loss of love with the dread of starvation. He suggested that the warmth, security and nourishment the infant experienced at his mother's breast, is the prototype of the gratification which is later experienced as self esteem.[84]

Rado believed the deepest fixation point in the depressive person is to be found in the hunger situation of the ungratified infant. As the "Oral-Narcissistic bliss" of the infant is dependent upon nourishment supplied by mother, so does the narcissistic gratification of the depressive depend upon love and appreciation from outside sources.

***

Freud believed that by putting food, the symbolic loved one, into his mouth and incorporating it, the melancholic was unconsciously fulfilling his wish to be magically one with his loved one.[85]

Eating the Pain Away

*O*vereating *is used by many to deal with a loss or severe disappointment and a resulting depressive reaction.* For the person who longs for a feeling of oneness with mother, overeating may unconsciously and symbolically harken back to a time with the nurturing mother of infancy, when a satisfied feeling of well being existed. To compensate for the feeling of loss or hopelessness, the overeater feels temporarily, blissfully nourished.

***

Overeating, precipitated by a depression due to a loss or bitter disappointment, may offer soothing and comfort when the person's own internal soothing mechanisms are deficient. The overeating functions as the mother of infancy and later as the transitional object of childhood did. The pain is temporarily assuaged through the soothing function of the food.

***

Overeating, following a loss, may unconsciously be acting out the rageful feelings toward the disappointing or abandoning person. The eating, unconsciously, is symbolically tearing the disappointing or abandoning person apart, devouring, digesting, and finally ejecting him as feces.

***

Sometimes depression, which is the consequence of a loss or harsh disappointment, signifies to the person, he is not in control. Overeating may reflect a symbolic action, assuring the person he is at least in total control of his body.

The loss of self-esteem and the feelings of helplessness and hopelessness to do anything about it, appear to be the primary feature of most depressive reactions. A loss of self esteem results when there is a discrepancy between what we wish ourselves to be and how we actually perceive ourselves. When this disparity exists, aggression, which is manifested by harsh self critical thoughts, is turned on oneself. This, in addition to a feeling of helplessness and hopelessness to repair the unsatisfactory self image, results in depression.

A person who is inclined toward depression will view the loss of a career promotion, not as a temporary setback or disappointment, but as reflective of his stupidity, lack of insightfulness, inadequacy, lack of lovablity or some other self criticism. He will berate himself for failing in the way he was berated, as a child, or more likely, he will chastise himself more harshly than anyone else ever had.

Someone who is depressed following the loss of someone he loves responds in a similar way. Instead of focusing on missing the loved person, as we would when mourning, the depressed person experiences self contempt. His focus may be that the person left him because he is not worthy of being loved or because he is ugly, wimpy, dull, etc. Upon analyzing his feelings, what is frequently revealed is that the contemptuous thoughts he has about himself, are actually feelings he has toward his abandoning loved one. This is why many people refer to depression as anger turned against oneself. In fact, accompanying the thought or act of suicide is often a fantasy of causing an abandoning person to feel hurt, guilty and sorry.

The loss of anything we overvalue regarding our feelings of self esteem, security and well being, can precipitate a depression. If our feeling of well being is predicated on love, money, power, status, fame, winning, beauty, strength, drugs, etc., the loss of it may result in depression and despair.

The depressed feeling resulting from the loss of anything we depend upon for our feeling of well being, does not necessarily lead to a depressive illness. The depressed feeling may act as a signal, which could result in countermeasures being invoked to stave off a depressive illness. The countermeasures we may employ can be healthy ones, like reevaluating our perception of our self and the situation which is causing our depressed feelings and developing a more positive, realistic and hopeful view and action. Other healthy countermeasures which our ego unconsciously invokes to avert a serious depression, are various defense mechanisms such as repression, rationalization, or intellectualization. Our ego summons these defenses to assist us in dealing with or mitigating the pain of our loss. Some common unhealthy countermeasures we use to assuage feelings of depression are alcoholism, drug addiction, and overeating. When countermeasures are not resorted to or fail, hopelessness, despair and more serious depression ensue.

***

Clearly, an individual's response to depressive reaction reflects unresolved and often unconscious issues from childhood. Depression or the attempt to fend off depression, may precipitate overeating as a way to assuage the pain of the depression. However, as we all know, overeating is just a temporary and inadequate solution.

Three

"No One Loves Me as I Want to Be Loved"

ost psychotherapists agree that the tendency towards depression is the result of early disappointments in the child's relationship with his parents. Edith Jacobson,[86] a psychoanalyst noted for her papers on depression, says that self esteem develops only in an atmosphere of parental love. When a child grows up in such an atmosphere, reasonable amounts of frustration and disappointment can be tolerated, and also promote the child depending on his own resources, which results in a child having a realistic understanding of what he can and cannot do. However, if a child suffers severe disappointments and frustrations too early in life or grows up in an atmosphere lacking in love, he will feel unvalued and unloved. He will identify with the critical judgements of his parents, which will result in a harsh critical superego and low self image.

If the child's experiences of lack of love occur before he has emotionally separated from his mother, his values and expectations of himself may be based on omnipotent fantasies he has about himself and his mother. Later on in life he may have unrealistic and extremely high expectations and demands of himself, reflecting his belief in his own omnipotence. Because these expectations are unrealistic, he will inevitably fail to achieve them. Consequently a great disparity would exist between the person he wishes to be and the person he perceives himself to be. This disparity may result in depression.

For example, consider the child who believes his mother is all powerful and all knowing. Because of factors existing in his early childhood, he has not been able to completely separate from her emotionally. Therefore, on some level, he believes there is no real boundary between himself and his mother. Consequently, he maintains the fantasy that he too is omnipotent. These thoughts and feelings are, undoubtedly, unconscious. Since this child and later adult harbors a fantasy of omnipotence, his expectations of himself will correspond with that fantasy. As an adult he will expect himself to achieve whatever he wishes. Because of the unconscious fantasy of omnipotence, any thought as to whether his wishes and expectations are realistic, would not exist.

This man may acquire a law degree and believe he will become a partner in the prestigious ABC law firm within two years. His belief may exist despite his knowledge that ABC's policy is that one cannot make partner before five years. This person's expectations of himself are inevitably doomed to failure. In two years when he has not made partner, this man may suffer a serious depression. Not only will he have failed to meet his ideal self, but he will feel helpless and hopeless to do anything about it.

A person who has more realistic expectations of himself may be disappointed he could not beat ABC's partnership policy, he may even have a slightly depressed reaction, but then, most likely, he would be able to reassess his goal and feel okay. Although this may be a harsh disappointment to this person's competitive spirit, it would not cause him to reproach himself or experience a sustained depression.

***

Karl Abraham believed that all major disappointments and depressive responses derived their importance from being representations of the child's original disappointment with his parents. He stated that the depressive's self reproaches were not only aimed at the abandoning love, but also the original disappointing parent.[87]

***

Several theorists believe that all of us go through a stage whereby we experience a state of "basic anxiety," which consists of sadness about disappointment regarding our loved ones, fear of losing them, and the longing to regain them. This is reflected in the thought: "no one loves me as I want to be loved." It is a feeling of being unloved, alone and helpless in a hostile world. These profoundly painful feelings evoke defenses or other restorative measures, such as *overeating*, to protect the person from such hurt.

***

The way this feeling of "basic anxiety" is successfully overcome is by internalizing, that is, taking in the love and feelings of security demonstrated to us by our parents, into our own inner self. However, when that love and positive regard is lacking, we, as children and later as adults, are vulnerable to continued anxiety and or depression. Then, because we do not have the inner feeling of being loved or valued, we are completely dependent on other people or things mirroring back to us that we are valuable. The lack of this positive reflection results in our low self esteem and perhaps depression.

Julia

Julia was a forty-two year old attractive, overweight lawyer. She was divorced and had custody of two teenage daughters. Julia had a long history of episodes of depression, none of which were severe enough for her to be treated with drugs. However, she acknowledged feeling seriously suicidal a few years before I began to see her.

Julia came to see me several months after the breakup of a love affair. She was feeling very depressed and exhibited signs of a clinical depression. She had difficulty getting out of bed in the morning and had to literally force herself to go to work. While working she manifested difficulty concentrating. She reported incessantly pondering why she was not good enough or loveable enough to sustain a love relationship. Julia related she had many love relationships during the seven years she was divorced, the ending of each and every one resulted in depression.

When a love relationship ended, Julia berated herself either for choosing the wrong man or being not interesting enough, not pretty enough or not loveable enough to sustain a good man's interest. The way she dealt with the pain of her depression was to overeat, and overeating exacerbated her depression. The more depressed she felt, the more she ate. The more she ate and the more weight she gained, the more depressed she would become. She would cruelly chastise herself for the weight gain, saying, "no wonder no one wants her, she wouldn't want her fat self either."

As her therapy progressed, her depression diminished and we were able to understand more about Julia's episodes of depression and overeating. Julia grew up in a lower middle class home with parents who did not demonstrate much affection toward her. Love was harshly withdrawn if she did not do exactly what they wished. She remembered her mother not speaking to her for a week at a time, whenever she talked back to her. That emotional abandonment was extremely upsetting and frightening for Julia. After experiencing it a few times, Julia made sure it never occurred again; she became a very compliant girl.

However, her compliance did not stop her parents from being very critical of her. Whenever she showed any interest in something they did not, they would criticize or ridicule her. Actually, her depressive episodes seem to have begun in childhood, although no one ever recognized them as such. Her mother would call her a sour puss, because she often appeared glum. She recalled a day in her teens when her parents forgot she was going on a trip with an aunt and did not know where she was. They called her friends and asked them if they knew of her whereabouts. They did not. Afterwards, her friends confided to Julia that they feared she had killed herself. So although no one acknowledged that Julia was struggling with serious emotional problems, her friends intuitively knew it.

Julia's mother was a volatile woman, who would explode when she was angry and abruptly leave the house for many hours at a time. Her mother's behavior was very frightening, as Julia believed her mother would never return. Julia did everything in her power to appease and please her mother. Nothing seemed to work.

When Julia's mother expressed affection and attention toward her, it was through preparing her special meals and snacks. Julia felt loved and taken care of at those times. For Julia food was equated with love.

Because Julia was not able to internalize that she was loveable, smart, interesting or joyful she did not experience herself in those ways. She deeply wished to be regarded as someone who was loveable and admirable, but believed she was lacking. Indeed, she had all those attributes and more. However, the only time Julia was able to acknowledge positive attributes about herself was when they were being reflected back from someone else. Consequently, when someone else paid attention to her and conveyed to her she was loveable and smart she would feel great. However, when that external response was absent, she would revert back to feeling inadequate. When she succeeded in achieving the goals she was striving for at work she would feel smart and successful. However, if a case she was working on did not work out well, she would feel completely inadequate and think about leaving law before she got fired. Julia was completely dependent on external supplies for her sense of self esteem.

Julia experienced every man she went out with as a potential someone who could help her feel more loveable: if only he loved her. What was important to Julia was the man fall in love with her; however, she was not discriminating about whether the man himself was loveable. Each time a relationship with a man broke up, she would condemn herself for being stupid because she chose the wrong man, or for being unlovable and therefore responsible for the breakup. Every breakup with a man echoed the old devastating feelings of abandonment by her mother. She would feel completely undesirable and believed abandonment would always be inevitable. Essentially, she believed she would never enjoy the happiness of a secure relationship; that was a special thing reserved for special people. It was at those times, when she felt completely hopeless and helpless, that she would think about suicide.

The only thing that mollified Julia's pain was eating. When Julia felt depressed, she would binge. She would eat every chance she had. Driving home from work she would stop at bakeries, candy stores, diners, pizza places, fast food restaurants and buy enough food for the drive home. At home she would prepare fattening enjoyable dishes, when she was functional enough to do so. If she was too depressed to cook, she would take her children out to eat in expensive restaurants and order and finish five course dinners, although at times she could ill afford to do so. When she finished dinner, she would either go to sleep or wait until her fullness desisted, so she could continue eating. When she ate she felt soothed, entitled and numb.

The day after the binge, Julia would feel depressed about all the weight she was sure she had gained. Being fat, she thought, would make her even less loveable. She would commit herself to diet and exercise; however, frequently, she would just continue to binge.

Through her work in therapy, Julia was able to develop a more realistic perception of herself. Her self image gradually changed as she was able to truly recognize that she *was* loveable, smart, interesting, joyful, and successful. Indeed, she was all she had wished to be. She realized that her dependence on a man to reflect back that she was loveable made her incapable of choosing a man who would be suitable for her. For she had not been choosing the man; she was just hoping the man would choose her. Furthermore, her need for a man's love caused her to behave in a very needy manner, something which adversely affected her relationships. Julia began to understand that because she did not have adequate internal resources to calm and comfort herself, she was using bingeing for that purpose. It was the way she soothed herself and brought about feelings of being nurtured. Over a period of time, Julia developed more appropriate ways to soothe and comfort herself when she was distressed.

Julia story has a happy ending. Recognizing her own wonderful qualities, she began to believe that a man would be lucky to have her as his mate. She became discriminating about whom she dated, realizing she wanted to date only the kind of men she felt would be suitable for her. Toward the end of her therapy, she had met and was planning to marry another lawyer who related to her with much love and respect. Her relationship with her fiancé was quite different than past relationships, as she was no longer needy and completely dependent on outside sources for approval.

Four

Hunger Pains

The realization that you eat because you are depressed is most likely not new to you. What probably has not been apparent before is what your overeating symbolizes and what function it serves for you. Although the symptom of depression which triggers overeating may be the same for many people, the function one's overeating serves may be different for different individuals. What purpose your overeating serves will depend on your particular unresolved issues from childhood. For example does your overeating serve to symbolically reunite you with your mother of childhood, or is its function to fill a feeling of emptiness, or does it serve to express anger and defy another's expectations? Think about what is truly causing you to feel depressed and what childhood issues are being stirred up because of it.

***

Think about how depressed you feel. How long have you been feeling depressed? Does your depression match the signs of a clinical depression: low mood, feeling of hopelessness, inability to sleep or sleeping too much, overeating, or lack of appetite, difficulty thinking or concentrating, low self esteem? If you believe you have symptoms which point to a clinical depression, you should seriously consider getting professional help.

***

If, through your exercises to develop awareness, you have become aware that you overeat when you are depressed in order to symbolically merge with your nurturing mother of infancy, use that awareness while doing the 10 minute exercise. Forestall your craving to overeat for 10 minutes. Use that time to think about why you want to overeat now. Acknowledge that the blissful nurturance you are longing for will be fulfilled, only temporarily, by eating. In fact, afterwards you will probably feel more depressed because of the bingeing.

While doing the 10 minute exercise think about the meaning of your planned overeating. If you recognize your eating is symbolically designed to angrily devour and destroy the person who hurt you, acknowledge that you are enraged at this person but there are much healthier ways to express that rage than overeating. Indeed, if you think about it, the only one your rageful eating bout is hurting is you. Express your rageful feelings to someone you can trust. Scream, cry, talk and talk and talk about it. Try punching a punching bag or a pillow to rid yourself of your painful rage. Go out for a brisk walk or run. Exercise. Play a fierce game of tennis or racquet ball and beat the hell out of the ball. Turn to some carrots or the like which you can chew and grind up the way you wish to ravage the person who hurt you.

Appreciate that the extent of the rage you feel toward this person may be exacerbated by rageful feelings which are remnants of childhood hurts and abandonments. During childhood we are completely dependent on others to provide nurturance, love and security. We are extremely vulnerable to hurt and pain when those fundamental needs are not provided for. When love and support is withdrawn from us as adults, it often echoes that time in our childhood when nurturance from our parents was so essential. Not that love and support are not important to all of us in the present; they are. However, we are no longer completely dependent on only one person to provide it.

Think about whether the people you depend upon for love and support are capable of providing it. If not, do not spend your time trying to change them, contemplate ways to develop healthier, more supportive relationships. Consider what you may be doing to possibly contribute to people disappointing you or abandoning you. By that I do not mean putting yourself down, but rather stepping back and trying to objectively see whether you are allowing people to treat you poorly. If so, plan to change that way of relating and, if necessary, with whom you maintain relationships.

Recall the people in your life who do give you love and support. Think of ways you can increase the love and support in your life. If you believe that no one is giving you the kind of love and support you need, reassess your need. Is it possible the people in your life are supportive, but your need for love and support is based on early childhood needs for complete nurturance, and therefore is unrealistic now?

Keep focusing on your goal of becoming thin; use your anger in a healthy way, turning its force and energy into fierce determination to become slim and to never allow anyone again to precipitate your hurting yourself.

Try to look at the event which precipitated your depression from another perspective. Attempt to think about the situation without any self critical thoughts. Think about how an objective person would perceive the situation. Turn to friends and family who are supportive and objective to help you with the painful feelings you are having. Assess whether your wishes and aspirations which have been thwarted are realistic. Plan a course of action that will bring about the achievement of realistic goals.

***

If you succeeded in forestalling your overeating for the <u>10 minute</u> exercise period, good for you! Let yourself feel the pleasure of that achievement. If you were able to divert your desire to overeat, and instead worked on resolving the real issue causing your depression, you did a superb job and deserve a reward. Plan to reward yourself with a bubble bath, a movie, a new outfit or whatever would please you. It is very important for you to do so.

Acknowledging your successes and positive attributes is essential for you to achieve positive emotional and physical health. Plus, it is much more pleasant and affirming than what many of us are proficient at: berating ourselves for any failing. Learn to easily recognize, acknowledge and reward your successes. Be determined to focus on what is positive about yourself and what you do. Allow yourself to be human: a good enough person who makes mistakes and suffers failures, but who also enjoys successes. It is absolutely crucial that you do not minimize or disparage each small victory you have. Each small victory is a step towards reaching your final goal; being slim.

***

If you were not able to succeed this time, it is essential that you do not chastise yourself. We all fail at times. None of us fulfills all our plans or commitments to ourselves. Be nice to yourself and reassure yourself that although you were not able to divert yourself from overeating this time, you will next time. Spend time thinking about what you will do to be more successful next time.

Eating never fills a
lonely heart.

Part Eight

Smorgasbord

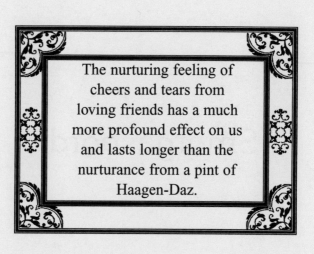

The nurturing feeling of cheers and tears from loving friends has a much more profound effect on us and lasts longer than the nurturance from a pint of Haagen-Daz.

One

Smorgasbord

L ana, the woman who said she wished she could be an elephant because elephants never leave their children, is obese. One reason she eats so much is to be certain she will never starve again. Another is to insure she is sexually undesirable, for Lana, from the age of five, was frequently, sexually abused. As a young girl Lana bartered for food with her body. But there is another reason Lana is fat. She wants to be fat. Remember, she always wanted to belong, to feel part of a family. Well, when she was twenty-two she was "adopted" by a nun who left the convent in which Lana was residing. Thereafter, Lana and the nun lived together. The nun became the "mother," Lana never had.

The nun and her family are obese. Lana wants to fit in by looking just like them and being just like them. Being fat allows her to feel as if she is part of their family, that she belongs. She has consciously identified with this family and wishes others to see her resemblance to them. Remember, as a child Lana hoped others would believe she was the daughter of women who were shopping. Her desire to belong is so strong, that being fat for Lana is not a negative attribute, rather it is an indicator she is loved and belongs to a family.

A heartwarming and interesting footnote to Lana's story is that although she is a few months older than the nun, the nun legally adopted her. This adoption was highly significant for both of them. It provided Lana with a mother whom the world would legally recognize as hers, and allowed the nun to have the daughter she would never have been able to have. Reportedly, the nun's adoption of Lana, the adoption of one adult by another, is a legal first.

Belonging, and the feeling of being loved, is profoundly important to all of us. We too, like Lana, consciously or unconsciously, identify with different attributes of people who are dear to us, including being overweight.

***

Another woman, Marie, kept herself 80 pounds overweight for exactly the opposite reason. Experiencing herself as fat and asexual separated her from her beautiful, slender, but overtly promiscuous mother. She was very ashamed to be the daughter of the woman who was the town "tramp" and wanted to be nothing like her. In addition, her overeating served another function, that of keeping her close to the fantasied nurturing mother of infancy.

***

Loss is always difficult and painful. Understandably, we frequently search for something to diminish the painful feeling of the loss. For many, eating can symbolically alleviate this painful feeling. Overeaters often overeat or binge when they have suffered the loss of a loved one, their self esteem or something else they value. Unconsciously, they are symbolically restoring the loss or soothing its pain. In the book, *Feeding the Hungry Heart*, a woman describes the feelings she had when her first love died, when she was in junior high school. "I tried to make death go away. I wooed it with fried chicken and crab salad, tried to smother it with rice pudding." Her eating, she says, was related to the wish to retrieve the loss she had suffered.[88]

***

For some, being fat serves as an excuse for not succeeding. Due to feelings of low self esteem, these people, often unconsciously, fear if they aspired to what they wished, they would fail. They protect themselves from failure by maintaining that their low achievement is related to their unacceptable appearance. Sometimes their fear is accurate because their aspirations are unrealistic. For instance, one woman believed if she lost weight every man in the world would desire her. She asserted the only reason she was not married to the most handsome, wealthy, and wonderful man in the world, was she just could not control her appetite. Her rationalization protected her from humiliation regarding her lack of omnipotence and inability to have whomever and whatever she wanted. Her bingeing symbolized her desire to have whatever and as much as she desired.

***

Donald discovered his obesity was related to symbolically swallowing his nurturing mother of infancy. This fantasy was one way he provided himself, albeit symbolically, with the nurturance for which he desperately longed. His obesity also served other functions as well: Donald wanted to outdo and be much more attractive than his father who was obese. Donald's own obesity served as a defense against that unconscious angry and competitive wish. In addition, his obesity functioned as a punishment for his wishes to angrily surpass and shame his father; Donald was even fatter than his father and was frequently subjected to ridicule. Donald used his obesity as an expression of rage toward his wife, who unconsciously represented his critical and withholding mother. His wife, who ultimately felt ashamed to be seen with him and repulsed looking at him, refused to have sex with him. In this way, she responded to his unconscious provocation to become the critical and withholding symbolic mother. Therefore, through obesity, Donald unconsciously maintained connected to and avoided the feeling of separation from, both his mother and father.

***

In addition to Diane's conscious knowledge that she was keeping herself fat to avoid sex because of its connection to childhood sexual abuse, she became aware of several other functions her obesity served. Her large protruding stomach unconsciously functioned to deny an abortion she had as a teen, something about which she felt very guilty. Unconsciously, she was still pregnant. Also, experiencing herself as ugly and undesirable protected her from feelings of envy from her mother, whom Diane believed, knew her father was abusing her. She believed her mother hated her because she was envious her father chose her over her mother. Her obesity was a way to demonstrate she did not wish to steal her father or triumph in any way over her mother. Her obesity resulted in her mother's concern and sympathy. Being obese also functioned as a punishment for agreeing to, and at times enjoying, having sex with her father.

***

From the cases illustrated, we can see that the underlying reason for being overweight is often multidetermined, having several interconnected causes. Someone who is fat because of his or her need to defy expectations may uncover that the overeating also functions as a soothing mechanism, supplanting a missing soothing ability. A person who is obese as a protection against envy may also overeat to recover the lost nurturing mother of infancy. Most likely there are several conscious and unconscious wishes that underlie a person's overeating, which is understandable, since we all passed through each developmental phase of childhood and may have remnants of the struggles of those phases. In addition, our adult lives have been filled with many experiences which evoke complex feelings and responses.

Two

Wonderful Connections

Beyond the stages of early childhood, many other things can be associated consciously and unconsciously with food and eating. Food and eating can symbolize a special person or time when love and happiness were felt. For instance, many people connect popcorn to fun times at the movies; hot dogs and peanuts are connected to exciting days at the ballpark. If those times at the movies and ballpark are associated with a special person who shared that special day, then popcorn or hot dogs may also be connected to that special person. Later on, food and eating may be used to deny the feeling of loss of that person who was in some way associated to food or the pleasure of eating. Or food may be used to retrieve the loving experiences that are connected to that person or emotion. To eat, then, is to regain unconsciously that lost person or loving, fulfilling experience.

***

Holiday meals exemplify eating that is connected to fond memories of special people and family gatherings. Holidays, such as Thanksgiving and Christmas, are often looked forward to as a way to relive happy times of childhood. Overeating at holiday times may be connected to happy fun times, when everyone in the family overate. This nostalgic feeling connected to food makes eating all the more pleasurable. It is a way to feel wonderfully nurtured both physically and emotionally.

Frequently, however, these meals, or the relationships surrounding the meals, are quite disappointing. It may be the happy remembered time was a fantasy, or a wish of what holiday times were, rather than what they truly were. Our memories of holiday meals may hark back to when we were very young and getting lots of special attention. What we may choose to forget, are the conflictual relationships that existed and were expressed.

Consequently, the attempt to revive that fantasied time, results in failure. This disappointment, due to the inability to rekindle happy memories, may itself bring about overeating. The eating serves to reconnect with those happy times or fantasies, as well to soothe the pain of disappointment and loss.

My husband prepares the entire Passover dinner; he is a very busy man yet insists on doing it all himself. The cooking and preparation take about a week for we have approximately thirty-five people at our Seder. In the past, when he seemed so pressed for time I would ask him why we did not just have the Seder meal catered? He said, "I would never do that. All these foods and smells, and even the pressure of time, bring back the time when I was young and with my mother, and she did all this. I remember the smells of the chicken fat, pot roast, potatoes, and chicken soup cooking in the kitchen, and the wonderful happy gleam in my mother's eyes as she cooked and prepared for the holidays. I could never give that up."

In fact, at the Passover Seder the food itself serves to reconnect us with past generations of Jews, from the slaves of Egypt on. We eat certain foods that symbolize what our ancestors did during their slavery in Egypt. We eat bitter herbs to remind us of the bitterness of our slavery. We eat charoset (a mixture of apples and honey, to resemble cement) to remind us of the mortar the slaves used in laboring for the Pharaoh. We dip food in salt water to remind us of the tears our ancestors shed in Egypt. And we eat matzah to remind us of the bread baked hurriedly (because it did not have time to rise) as we swiftly left the slavery of Egypt.

***

There are many stories told about how generous and loving a man my grandfather was. (I never met him. He died before I was born. But I am named after him.) As I have said before, my mother and several of her siblings, are obese. Ever since I was a little girl, she has told me with great pleasure, that her father used to put chocolate under the pillows of all his children every night. He worked late and did not come home in time for his children to see him. To let them know he was thinking about them, he would buy each of them a candy bar and put it under their pillows. With this loving gesture, he would leave something sweet to remind them he loved them. My mother said the candy bar was usually squashed and melted from their sleeping on it, but that did not matter. Waking up and finding the chocolate was a highlight of her day. She and her siblings loved their father very much. The chocolate made my mother feel very much connected to him when he was gone. You will not be surprised to know my mother loves chocolate. For her, chocolate is love.

***

Roseanne Barr, in her book Roseanne, *My Life as a Woman*, connects food with her Bubbe, her grandmother, whom she loved and greatly admired. Speaking about her grandmother she said. "You came here for tea, refuge, conversation, warmth, a game of gin rummy (which she always won); you came here to snoop in the closets (where she stored the wine she made herself from her grape arbor in the backyard), you came for a bagel, or soup, or to steal quarters out of her purse, to play in the junked cars she had in her backyard, or to go through the shed . . . . I loved my grandmother more than any other human being because she never lied, never told you what you wanted to hear, never compromised . . . . One of her great talents was her cooking, which consisted of exciting things to do with fats . . . she made a salad that was so incredible, and her spaghetti is still, to this day, untopped. You were never allowed in the cooking process, only to follow her and clean up or chop walnuts or peel potatoes."[89]

***

I have many fond memories of my mother conveying her love to me through food. Frequently, when I came home from elementary school, my mother was baking. I can still remember those wonderful smells of cookies and cakes baking in the oven. I especially loved when she would let me help her bake. At those times, I felt so special, grown up and connected to her. After she frosted the cake, she would let me lick the frosting bowl. I would stick my finger in the bowl, swirling it around and around until it was completely covered with frosting. And then, to add to my joy, I sat there, with her approval, sucking each morsel of frosting off of my finger. That was ecstasy! A truly marvelous feeling.

When I was a little older, sometimes she wasn't home when I returned from school. She was either working at an occasional job, or was playing canasta or Mah Jong with "the girls." On those occasions, she always left me a treat. Just like her father left chocolate for her when he wasn't home, I would find a home made jelly apple, home baked cupcakes or cookies on the kitchen table. Because of the gifts she left me, her absence was less difficult. I remember seeing the treats on the table and feeling her love. My mother had difficulty expressing her love in any other way. So love for me was intimately connected to food.

When I was younger, there were times when it felt terrible returning home from school. Not only was my mother not home, but I couldn't get into my apartment. My mother would not give me a key, because she did not want others to think I was a "latch-key child." At those times, I would wait in the hallway of our apartment building for her to come home. Seeing me standing outside my locked door, sometimes my friend, who lived on the same floor as we did, invited me to come into her apartment and wait for my mother. I remember it as if it were yesterday. I would salivate in anticipation of my friend offering me some cookies and milk, or some gum drops which were always on the living room table. Even today, each time I see gum drops I think fondly of my friend. Eating was the thing that relieved my missing and hunger for my mother. It unconsciously and symbolically restored my mother to me. Clearly, eating for me is connected to feelings of emotional reassurance and love. And not surprisingly, my thoughts often turn to food when I am confronted with something painful. Eating assuages the pain for me, because it symbolically brings back times when I felt safe and loved by my mother.

Three

Losing Weight Versus the Feeling of Invulnerability

When we overeat it is not only other people whom we seek to unconsciously restore. The same dynamic can operate unconsciously to restore the loss of anything, even the loss of the sense of one's physical self.

People begin psychotherapy because they want to feel better. However, at times they interfere with the psychotherapeutic process because they are afraid of change. Consciously they may want to change, but unconsciously their wish may be to remain the same, because changing may mean giving up too much that is familiar. What is familiar may be painful, nonetheless, it may be what is unconsciously sought, because at least it is known.

With patients who regress by overeating following a period of progress, I talk about the pictures used in advertisements for weight loss programs. In these advertisements you typically see a picture of the person before the weight loss. Next to the "before" picture, you see another picture of the person following the weight loss. Because the weight control program wants to show off its most successful cases, the advertisement often illustrates this with photographs of people who were very obese before and thin now. These pictures often exhibit people who have lost a hundred pounds or more. What is reflected is an incredible difference in appearance. Actually, if you think about it, the amount of weight lost can equal the weight of an entire person!

What is especially significant, however, is another loss: the loss of the self image of the person who lost all this weight. The person in the "before" picture is gone, yet she is the one whom the dieter has known for most of her life. Even though this slender image may be exactly what has been wished for a lifetime, it is often quite traumatic. Who is this new, thin person in the mirror? It certainly is not the reflection of the self image this person has always known. Even if hated, the lost image is often unconsciously sought again, because it is familiar and comfortable. The unconscious desire to revive the old and comfortable image often results in renewed overeating. In this way, the dieter reverses the unbearable loss, and retrieves a familiar self image and all that it connotes.

***

A striking observation was made in a study assessing the response of obese patients to their weight loss. The subjects of this study were hospitalized an average of eight months and lost an average of 86.7 lbs. Nevertheless, these individuals' perception of themselves negated their weight loss. They experienced themselves as having lost no weight or just a slight amount of weight. They maintained a "phantom body size" phenomenon. The authors suggest there may be psychodynamic determinants for the maintenance of the perception of an obese body image.[90]

Obesity, for some, signifies strength, greatness, bigness, uniqueness, and invulnerability. Obesity may also serve exhibitionistic tendencies. Another study which evaluated the response of twenty-five obese individuals following their weight loss demonstrated that several of the dieters became depressed, believing they were now physically weak, helpless and vulnerable. Associated with those feelings was terror others would inflict harm upon them; that they would be unable to do physical tasks; and that the huge body image which enabled them to maintain isolation, was now lacking and undermining their feeling of being protected from emotional hurt and abandonment.[91]

For others, obesity served to rationalize social and sexual inhibitions. Once the obesity was not evident, several individuals felt truly threatened or defended against that threat by continuing to experience themselves as obese, through "the phantom body size" phenomenon.

Four

The Unthinkable and Unspeakable

S ome victims of childhood sexual abuse become promiscuous. Some become perpetrators of sexual abuse when they are adults; others fear and avoid sex because of its connection to the abuse. *Overeating and maintaining an undesirable appearance function for many as a way to avoid sex. Obesity serves to reassure these victims that the guilt, pain, and fear they suffered as children will not have to be reexperienced, because they are not sexually desirable.*

"Soul Murder,"[92] is the phrase Leonard Shengold, M.D. coined to describe sexual abuse perpetrated against another. The victims of "soul murder" experience a terrible and terrifying combination of helplessness and rage. These feelings are so unbearable they must be suppressed or repressed for the person to emotionally survive. Children are the usual victims of "soul murder" because they are completely physically and emotionally dependent on adults and therefore cannot escape their torturer. The child must submit to and often identifies with the abuser.

The act of sexually abusing anyone is reprehensible. It inevitably leaves the victim with permanent emotional scars. The victims of sexual abuse frequently maintain feelings of guilt and responsibility for the act. The feeling of shame about being violated in this way is so profound, often the victim does not tell anyone about the abuse. The victim suffers in silence, suppressing the memory of the act and suffering its ramifications, unable to resolve the overwhelming feelings. Or the victim may review the traumatic experience over and over as a shameful, punishing, anxiety and guilt provoking videotape.

Frequently, the child represses the memory of the abuse because the trauma is too much to bear. Nevertheless, the ramifications of the abuse manifest itself in later life, often leading the victim to seek out help, as an adult, for a seemingly unrelated problem. Whether or not the sexual abuse is remembered, its occurrence leaves profound emotional scars.

Sexual abuse perpetrated on a child evokes many conflictual feelings. Initially, it may be experienced by the child as loving and pleasurable, since all children desire love and affection from their parents. Ultimately, the child feels confusion, anxiety, guilt, fear, as well as overstimulation and pain. This frightening mixture of overstimulation and pain results in rage and both sexual and aggressive feelings. Often "brainwashing" of the child takes place, in which the child is frightened into believing that something terrible will happen to him or her, or to parents or loved ones if he or she tells anyone what has happened.

The abuse, especially if perpetrated on a child whose self image is not completely consolidated, negatively affects the victim's self image, ability to trust, relationships, sexual or otherwise, and often severely affects his or her attitude towards life in general. Every victim of sexual abuse with whom I have worked believed that their husband, wife, family or friends would view them in a devalued way if they knew of the abuse, even though many who were abused as children maintained the intellectual belief, they were not responsible for the abuse. Most victims of child abuse inevitably reveal, on some level they believe they were guilty of causing the abuse. They believe if they were not such cowards and said no or told a family member or clergy or teacher, this would not have happened. They believe if they were not so unlovable and therefore longing for any kind of love or touch, this would not have occurred. It usually takes a long time for victims of childhood sexual abuse to work through the complicated feelings and thoughts they have about the abuse, so that it ceases to have a negative impact on their lives.

***

A woman I treated, who was sexually abused as a child, panicked every time anyone noticed she lost some weight. Her immediate thought was someone would soon desire her sexually. Her response to that thought was to eat as much as she could, as eating and being fat made her feel secure she was sexually undesirable.

***

Another woman I treated, who was a victim of sexual abuse as a child, not only kept herself obese to avoid the attention of men, but slept in her clothes. She believed her clothes would give her a chance to defend herself, in case of a rape attempt. She also wanted to make sure there was no event, such as a fire during the night, whereby anyone would have a chance to see her in her pajamas or underwear, the clothes she wore when her father abused her.

***

Being obese functions as a way to avoid intimacy for many victims of childhood sexual abuse. Because of the abuse, these people often fear being intimate with and trusting a partner. Obesity helps them feel protected from both physical and emotional closeness. They maintain the belief that no one would want to get too close to someone so unattractive. Also, their size literally precludes anyone from getting too close. One woman told me she needs to make sure to keep people at a distance for fear, if they got too close and friendly, they may touch her and feel her rolls of fat. Preserving her rolls of fat protected her from intimacy and kept her feeling safe.

Five

Separating Trauma from Sexuality

Being fat as a protection against experiencing feelings and thoughts connected with sexual abuse is not uncommon. Victims of sexual abuse often suffer from painful memories, anxiety, depression, guilt, fear, humiliation, low self esteem, as well as sexual difficulties. Some victims of sexual abuse have repressed the event and, therefore, do not remember it; however, that lack of memory does not protect the victim from the terrible feelings associated with being abused. To regain feelings of self esteem and happiness, as well as to resolve fears related to sexuality, the experience of the abuse must be resolved.

It is vital to acknowledge that a child is not responsible and therefore not guilty of anything, if that child engaged in a sexual act with an adult. That fact is true even if the child complied with or even wished to have that sexual activity. As we discussed before, children have all sorts of wishes but they do not have the ability to make responsible decisions. Adults have that responsibility.

Resolving fears of sexuality, as well as other feelings related to being abused which are contributing to overeating, necessitates that the traumatic situation and the associated feelings be separated from healthy sexual desires and present reality. Since this trauma is fraught with so many complicated feelings, it may be best to consult with a professional or an abuse victims group to deal with all the feelings that need to be resolved.

***

In addition, use the 10 minute exercise to forestall eating anything which would undermine your wish to be thin. Keep in the forefront of your mind your wish to be thin. Recognize that being thin and sexually desirable will not result in sexual activity unless you desire it to. Most likely the trauma that took place occurred when you were a child, unable to comprehend or control what was happening to you. You were not able then as you are now, to handle and protect yourself from unwanted sexual attention. Recognize you are now capable of taking care of yourself and deciding whether and when and with whom you wish to have sex. Acknowledge there is no reason for you to feel guilty about any sexual abuse which was perpetrated against you. Again, becoming thin does not mean you have to ever have sex again, if you do not wish to. But what it does mean is that you can be pleased with how you look, be healthier and have greater self esteem.

***

Do not forget to give yourself a lot of praise and a reward if you succeeded in putting off your desire to overeat. Acknowledge you did a great job and deserve it! Reassure yourself that you can be safe from sexual abuse even if you are thin and attractive.

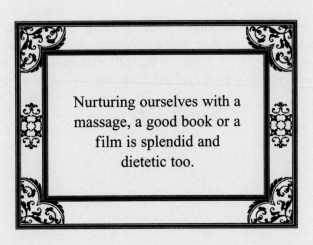

Nurturing ourselves with a
massage, a good book or a
film is splendid and
dietetic too.

Part Nine

Furthermore . . .

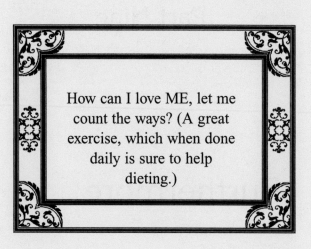

How can I love ME, let me count the ways? (A great exercise, which when done daily is sure to help dieting.)

One

Developing Awareness

Throughout this book we have observed how wishes of which we are not even aware, can profoundly affect our lives. How can we become aware of those wishes which exert a detrimental effect on us? I suggest in addition to rereading the chapters and cases in this book with which you identified or which made you feel uncomfortable, try the following exercise.

Sit or lie down in a comfortable position. Make sure your head is supported. Take a deep breath and let it out. Do that three times and then breathe normally. Focus on your head and tense your head as tight as you can for a few seconds. Then let it go completely limp. Next, focus on your forehead. Tighten your forehead as much as you can and then let it go as limp as you possibly can. Continue tightening and releasing every part of your body from your eyebrows to your toes, one part at a time. By the time you have let go of all the tension in your toes you should feel completely limp. Allow yourself to feel completely limp and deeply relaxed.

In that deeply relaxed state picture yourself as thin as you would like to be and dressed the way you always dreamed you could. Concentrate on that picture and focus on the feelings and thoughts that arise. Initially, the only thought you may have is that you look great and wish you could really look that way. Continue visualizing yourself thin; other thoughts may occur. Begin to see yourself thin and with your family. What thoughts occur now? Think of yourself thin and with your husband, boyfriend, (wife or girlfriend) and friends. Pay attention to what you imagine others reactions are to your slender appearance. What is your inner response to their reaction? In this fantasy how do you react towards them? Is there a discrepancy between your inner reaction and the way you imagine responding to them? If so, think about why that is?

Do this exercise once every day for several weeks. It may yield surprising thoughts if you truly allow yourself freedom of thought. Continue to do this exercise as you proceed with your diet, as new thoughts and feelings may arise each time you do it.

***

When you do identify thoughts you were not completely aware of before, write them down. Keep a journal of all these thoughts. I suggest this as an excellent way for you to know you experienced this thought, so later you will be less likely to disavow it. When thoughts are threatening, we all have the inclination to disavow them. Think about what you have written in your journal. If you have the inclination to disregard or even erase what you have written down, believing it is inaccurate, forget that! That inclination is probably indicative of a tendency to disavow uncomfortable thoughts. Do not erase or cross out any thoughts you have written down. These thoughts are important clues to understanding why you keep yourself overweight.

Think about your family dynamics connected to the thoughts you have written down. Think about what in your childhood may have resulted in these thoughts. Think about how these thoughts and connected feelings may affect your issues about food and eating. Think about this new awareness over a period of days, weeks and even years. Continue forever to be as aware as you can of what you think, feel and wish. The more we are aware of ourselves, the greater ability we have to be in control of what we consciously wish. If you can, talk to friends or family about what you are learning and thinking. Their response may reinforce what you are learning and even provide you with additional insight. It is important to write down or tape record all the new awareness you are gaining. Doing so will facilitate your continued development of self awareness.

Two

The Quest for the Perfect Body

Most people who want to be thinner have a reasonable body image in mind; that is, they merely wish not to be fat. However some people, especially women, do not have a reasonable body image in mind during their quest for a slimmer body. The body image they desire may range from emaciated, as in the case of an anorexic, to being what most people would regard as too thin. This can be a serious problem. Anorexics are people who have a distorted body image and view themselves as fat, even when they weigh eighty pounds and are hospitalized because their lives are at risk. In the hospital they are fed intravenously because although they are told they probably will die if they do not eat, they often will not. Many anorexics do die.

However, distorted body images are not limited to anorexics. The large percentage of people who acknowledge Bulimia, that is, throwing up their meals to stay thin or exercising 4-6 hours a day, after bingeing, attest to that. Many look in the mirror at a slender body and see a fat body. This distortion brings about much unnecessary anguish and low self esteem. Madison Avenue's high-style designers and Hollywood have created a model of a body image that is very thin and extremely difficult to maintain without incurring a serious eating disorder or feeling very deprived and depressed.

We are told by *Cosmopolitan, Elle* and *Vogue* how to have a perfect body. Women continually focus on the imperfections of their bodies thinking about how they could rearrange them through fasting, exercise, or surgery, so they will be perfect. Since we all have our own unique and therefore, in my opinion, beautiful bodies, our bodies resist grand scale rearranging. Why do we need to have perfect bodies? Why can't we have bodies that are good enough, slender enough, and beautiful enough?

This is a plea for exactly that! Let us all strive towards working on losing the weight we need to in order to be healthy and look well, but not perfect. Perfection always eludes those who seek it, anyway. It is incredibly difficult to maintain a weight of 108 if you are 5 feet 5 inches tall. You may be able to, but probably at the cost of constantly feeling deprived.

Ask yourself why you need to have a perfect body. Ponder the answers. Those answers must be really important to be worthy of your feeling continually deprived. I cannot imagine what might be so important. Some might say having a <u>perfect</u> body is the only way they will be loved by the kind of person they wish to be loved by. First of all, that is not true! Secondly, if the person you wish to be loved by desires you only if you look a particular way, one which causes you intense feelings of deprivation, is that love?

This is a plea to view yourself and your body more realistically. Determine what you would like to weigh and what size you would like to be. But please make sure your determination is based on what would contribute to your physical and <u>mental</u> health. Most of us are not going to walk down a fashion runway in the near future. We do not have to look as if we are. Lets aim for being and looking GOOD ENOUGH, not perfect.

Three

Diet and Exercise

" osing weight is as easy, intellectually speaking, as falling off a log. . . . Here it is, folks, the two-step program . . .

(1) Eat less.
(2) Exercise.

"I could tart it up for you, talk about fat grams, complex carbohydrates, aerobic capacity, waist-to-hip ratios, lactate thresholds, but the truth is, you don't need to know about all that. I have done it for you, read the books, followed the plans; I have kept food and exercise diaries, worked on my maximum oxygen uptake, lifted weights, read package labels.

"And here's what I learned . . . . You lock the door to your kitchen. You buy sneakers, go outside and you run; or else you row, row, your boat or ski cross-country or get on your bike. And you do these things consistently, again and again and again . . . and again . . . over a long period of time. The weight melts away . . . . Anybody can do this.

"All you have to do is master your craving for ice cream. Your dependence on double martinis. Your taste for Oreos and Snickers bars . . . . Give up the most reliable, most intense, most satisfying pleasure in life, a slice of cheesecake. Then find an hour or so every day or two in your insanely stressed-out frenzied, deeply problematic life . . . to work out.

"The weight came off gradually, kicking and screaming. I hit plateaus, weeks where nothing changed but my mood. I lapsed from time to time. but I never lost sight of the goal.

"Long live vanity! . . . looks became a symbol. I was still boss, if only of myself . . . . You need to be permanently vain because there is a downside to all this. Going hungry makes you irritable, and you have to go hungry. Eat All You Want And Lose Weight Fast, the ads say. Don't you believe it.

"You have to turn down the cheese-and-crackers, refuse the piece of chocolate cake from Zabar's, ...You may have done it, but you're not done. You cannot get off the bike or resupply your freezer with Cherry Garcia. Staying thin is a lifestyle. Every year something like 80 million Americans lose weight. Within five years, 95% of them have gained it back. You must make a habit of exercise and self denial.

"So you can never again indulge your appetite, except on isolated occasions. But that air of moral superiority you will carry around with you will more than make up for it. When you see an article in the paper about 'America's weight problem,' you will smile to yourself. What weight problem?"

This is an except of an article written by Anthony Brandt, in *Forbes FYI*, May 6, 1996. He wrote this article expressing his pride after keeping off the 50 pounds he lost and kept off for one year.[93]

***

Mr. Brandt conveys well what it takes to lose weight and keep it off, and I sincerely wish him well. <u>HOWEVER, he has disregarded an essential factor in maintaining weight loss. The crucial factor involved in maintaining weight loss is resolving the underlying issues that cause you to be fat in the first place.</u>

***

I am not going to elaborate what in particular you should eat to lose weight, other than making sure that you have enough of the daily nutrients your body requires. Briefly, the USDA currently recommends the following daily diet:

A Guide to Daily Food Choices

KEY   F= Fat (naturally   **S=** Sugars
occurring   (added)
and added)

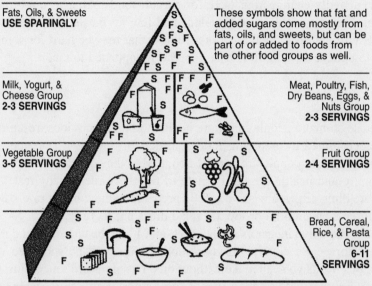

Fats, Oils, & Sweets
USE SPARINGLY

These symbols show that fat and
added sugars come mostly from
fats, oils, and sweets, but can be
part of or added to foods from
the other food groups as well.

Milk, Yogurt, &
Cheese Group
2-3 SERVINGS

Meat, Poultry, Fish,
Dry Beans, Eggs, &
Nuts Group
2-3 SERVINGS

Vegetable Group
3-5 SERVINGS

Fruit Group
2-4 SERVINGS

Bread, Cereal,
Rice, & Pasta
Group
**6-11
SERVINGS**

SOURCE: U.S. Department of Agriculture / U.S. Department of Health and Human Services

The less fat there is in the food choices you make, the more certain your body will use the fat from your body for its needs, and, therefore, the more certain you will be to lose weight. Of course, a low fat diet is not only essential for losing weight, but very important for maintaining good health. A high fat diet has been implicated in heart disease and several types of cancer. A low fat diet also allows us to eat more food than we normally would be able to eat when dieting. There are several books, available in your local book stores, which indicate the fat content as well as caloric content of most foods, including foods served in restaurants. It is a good idea to keep one of these available around meal times.

***

Other than making sure your diet is low in fat and you are eating enough of the basic nutrients your body needs, you should follow a diet that you like. You can make up your own, or use one of many available in diet books, magazines, or diet centers. You will be more likely to stay on a diet, lose weight and keep it off, if you do so slowly by changing your eating habits permanently. You will have a greater likelihood of success if your diet consists of things you like. However, you can, and many people have, actually change your taste for certain foods. After a long time of eating fresh vegetables, fruits, salads and low fat meals, fatty and sweet foods will not taste good anymore. I know that may be hard for some of you to believe now, but it is true. I swear, it happened to me.

***

Because so many people today are health and diet conscious, restaurants are accustomed to preparing food to order for anyone who requests it. More and more people are careful about what they eat, for both reasons of vanity and health. Do not hesitate to tell the waiter in any restaurant you are dining in, you wish your food prepared without butter or oil. Most restaurants have no fat or low fat salad dressing; feel free to ask for it. I, myself, use only vinegar as a salad dressing. I like the taste of it and it has zero calories. Be creative in your cooking. You will be surprised what delicious meals you can make without oils. I use mustard sauce, (just mix a tasty mustard with a little water to form a paste) or tomato sauce made only from canned stewed tomatoes and added spices, on chicken and fish, and have wonderful very low fat meals. If you add plenty of stewed, steamed or broiled vegetables, you will add to the taste and will get all those wonderful nutrients in as well.

***

In addition to eliminating fat in your diet, you must expend more calories than you take in, if you want to lose weight. You do not have to enroll in a gym or work out for hours if you do not wish to, but you do need to move. Actually, walking is the best exercise. It provides aerobic movement to strengthen your cardiovascular system, as well as uses energy, in other words, calories. If you are not fit and have not exercised in a long time start by walking. Begin your walking exercise at as comfortable a pace as you like. Make sure to walk at least 30 minutes at least 3 times a week. As you become more comfortable walking, speed up the pace until you are walking as vigorously as you can. It is beneficial to increase your exercise time, if you can, to 45 minutes, at least 3 times a week. In time, try to increase the frequency of your exercise time to 5 days a week.

Some people love to exercise. I hate to, but I do, because I want to keep my weight down and my strength up. Since I find exercising very boring, I do it in front of the television. I walk around my living room and dining room while I watch the news, a good movie or a lively video. When the weather is beautiful, I drive to a scenic spot and walk, often with a friend to make the walk more interesting.

Be creative and discover a method to insure you will exercise, be it walking in front of the television, out on a track, walking around the block, roller skating, cross country skiing, swimming, biking, rowing or anything else that uses energy. This is a must, so find an energy using exercise that you like and <u>do it.</u>

Get to know your body and its response to the reduction of calories through dieting and exercise. Some people lose weight immediately when they begin to diet. Others do not lose weight for several weeks, even though they are adhering strictly to their diet. Some people, although consistently on a diet and exercise regime will lose weight for two or three weeks and than lose nothing or even gain a few pounds for several more weeks. This inevitably evokes discouragement. It is <u>imperative</u> that you do not become discouraged and discard your diet program. Just as each of us have a different appearance, our metabolism and propensity for our cells to store fat differ. Eventually, if you remain on your diet program, you will become more slender, and pleased with your appearance.

Four

Getting Help

Many people, while recognizing the underlining dynamics that exist to keep themselves fat, are unable to resolve their conflicts on their own. Often, it is quite difficult to resolve deep seated and long lasting conflicts by ourselves, not because we are weak or inadequate, but because it is difficult to be objective about ourselves. If you find that to be true, it may be a good idea to get some professional or organized help. There are different ways to pursue such help. Since I am a psychotherapist and have helped many people with their internal conflicts, my bias is in favor of working these issues out in individual therapy, with a competent therapist; which is the way I worked through my own personal issues. I believe individual psychotherapy or psychoanalysis to be the most comprehensive way to deal with conflicts, especially if they are unconscious and long lasting.

In regard to individual psychotherapy as a method to resolve emotional problems of people who are overweight, one study followed eighty-four obese patients undergoing psychoanalysis for a period of four years. At the end of the study, sixty-six percent of the patients followed demonstrated a 40 pound or more weight loss. The researchers indicated the weight loss was generally well maintained and the patient's level of stress was diminished. Most importantly, psychoanalysis had a favorable impact on the patient's negative body image and feelings of inadequacy manifested prior to treatment. A greater acceptance of body image was associated with an increase in self esteem. The researchers concluded psychoanalysis was more effective in treating the issues of these obese individuals than other forms of psychological treatment.

***

To locate a competent psychoanalytically trained psychotherapist contact psychoanalytic institutes in your area and/or the Society of Clinical Social

Workers, The American Psychological Association, or The American Psychiatric Association.

***

Individual therapy is not the only method that can effectively assist overweight people. Many people get help working on their emotional issues in group psychotherapy. It is important to find a group that is insightful but supportive. The best way to find a group is through recommendations of friends, a local university or any of the above mentioned associations.

***

Self help groups, such as Overeaters Anonymous have also been very helpful to many. They often are based on a buddy system, whereby all group members are encouraged to talk to their sponsor or buddy when they feel the desire to overeat or when they are upset about something else going on in their lives. The emotional support of a peer who is undergoing similar struggles is helpful to many. Diet centers such as the Diet Center, Jeannie Craig Personal Weight Management and Weight Watchers, have helped many people with motivation, nutrition counseling, and diet supervision.

***

Whatever method you try, do not give up. Remember the issues and conflicts underlying your overeating have been in existence a long time, so it may take some time to work them out. But do not let that discourage you. It is absolutely essential you do not give up hope. If you persevere and continue to work on yourself, getting help if you need it, you will ultimately succeed in making your wish to be slender come true. If one therapist or group is not helpful, try another. I am certain if you do not give up, you will get the help you need and will overcome your problem of overeating. I have confidence in you. You must, too.

***

Feel free to write to me about your progress and experience losing weight. I am interested in you and how you are doing.

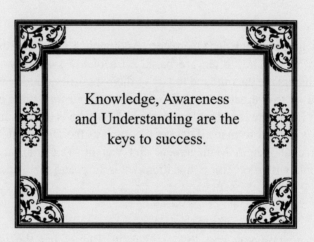
Knowledge, Awareness
and Understanding are the
keys to success.

Glossary

Ambitendency: Initially referring to a toddler in the rapproachment phase of child development, ambitendency reflects the simultaneous desire to be united with one's mother and separate from her.

Anal character: A term used to describe a person whose personality reflects characteristics such as frugality, obsessiveness, stinginess, orderliness, excessive ambivalence, messiness, defiance and sadomasochistic inclinations, which are believed to be derived from conflicts surrounding the anal phase of life.

Anal period: The phase of child development occurring between ages one to three, characterized by the child's pleasure focused on his anus and his newly developed ability to control his sphincter.

Anorexia Nervosa: An eating disorder characterized by the obsessive quest for thinness and the dread of being fat. The anorexic typically has a distorted image of her/his body and is capable of seeing a fat body when looking in the mirror at an actual eighty pound body. A serious case of anorexia nervosa can be fatal.

Anxiety: A very distressing feeling related to a sense of impending danger.

Anxiety Disorder: A psychopathological condition whereby anxiety, consciously experienced or not, is the central feature. This condition usually manifests in unrealistic worry, fear of imminent danger, irritability, restlessness, feeling shaky and the feeling of tenseness.

"As-if" personality: A severe personality disorder characterized by a tendency to imitate and be like the person one is with at the moment. Although the person with an "as-if" personality may reflect an appearance of involvement with another, there is actually a lack of authenticity to what the person expresses.

Autonomy: The state of being independent and capable of emotionally and physically functioning on one's own. Autonomy usually refers to a sense of self-determination and direction.

Boundary: The awareness of a distinction between the self and another.

Bulimia: An eating disorder characterized by the quest for thinness and the fear of being fat. Bulimia, also referred to as anorexia bulimia is manifested by food binges followed by regurgitation or laxative use.

Characterological: Relating to fixed personality traits of an individual.

Compromise Formation: A compromise manifested by a symptom, a behavior, a personality trait, or other pattern, which emerges to substitute for a wish or impulse which is barred from consciousness, because it is deemed unacceptable by the ego or superego.

Displacement: A defense mechanism characterized by the shifting of attention from one idea or thing, onto another which is more acceptable. For example, in a dream hostile feelings expressed towards a neighbor, may be a displacement from hostile feelings towards a parent. This displacement permits the avoidance of anxiety which would ensue if the anger toward the parent was recognized.

Ego: One of the three parts of our mind. The other two are the id and the superego. Freud designated the term ego to represent that part of the mind which deals with the world outside ourselves. The ego also mediates between the two other parts of our mind, the superego, which reflects moral demands, and the id, which reflects instinctual strivings. The ego evaluates the needs of the self through its functions of perception, intention, anticipation, thinking, reality testing, and frustration tolerance, just to name a few. The ego develops and maintains defensive functions such as repression, projection, rationalization, and intellectualization.

Enmeshment: A situation in which two or more people are emotionally entangled, prohibiting each from functioning optimally and independently.

Erotogenetic zones: Those anatomical areas of the body which, if stimulated, evoke sexual feelings. These areas of the body are genetically determined, but may be influenced by environmental factors.

False Self: A state of being whereby a person hides his true self from others and/or himself. Everyone has a social self which covers up one's true self. The degree of use of the false self is significant, with regard to psychopathology. The most extreme case of the false self is the "as-if" personality.

Fantasy: A wish dramatized in one's imagination.

Fixation: A primary way of relating to the world that is based on an earlier stage of childhood development. For example, someone who is fixated at the oral developmental stage will relate in terms of wanting to be fed, perhaps literally by overeating, and/or continually wanting to be fed with affection, compliments, attention, etc.

"Good enough" mother: A term coined by Donald Winnicott, M.D., a pediatrician turned psychoanalyst, which refers to a mother's intuitive and active adaptation to her child's needs. The "good enough" mother's adaptation diminishes with the child's growing ability to tolerate frustration.

Id: One of the three parts of the mind. The other two are the ego and the superego. The id reflects our innate and instinctual wishes to gratify our fundamental needs.

Impulse: An irresistible desire to take an action, usually erotic or aggressive in nature.

Individuation: The unfolding of the child's own unique characteristics. Individuation is part of the process of separation-individuation whereby the child recognizes that he is distinct from his mother and is different from her as well.

Instinctual: Urges or behavioral drives presumed to be genetically derived. The expression of those urges are mediated by the environment and the person's ego and superego.

Intellectualization: A defense mechanism characterized by a focus on philosophical or abstract discussions which functions to avoid conflictual ideas or feelings.

Internalization: Through the ego's functions of perception, memory, and symbolization, relationships with others are preserved by making them part of the self. Internalization functions to assuage the feeling of loss.

Obsessive-Compulsive Disorder: A psychopathological condition whereby one consistently experiences an obsession or compulsion which causes him distress and interferes with his optimal functioning. Obsessions are persistent thoughts, urges, or images which the person has no control over. Compulsions are repetitive intentional behaviors which are performed according to certain rules and respond to an obsession.

Oedipus Complex: Referring to that stage in child development, from approximately three to six years of age, when a child maintains the wish to be the lover of the parent of the opposite sex and be rid of its rival, the parent of the same sex. Coexisting with these wishes are desires for the same sex parent and rivalrous feelings toward the parent of the opposite sex. The child fears retaliation for these incestuous wishes and renounces them by identifying with the parent of the same sex.

Omnipotence: The belief of having complete power which knows no bounds.

Phobia: A disorder characterized by the avoidance of certain things or situations in order to avoid extreme anxiety. Many people who suffer from a phobia experience intense anxiety merely thinking about encountering the dreaded situation.

Psychic determinism: A fundamental tenet of psychoanalysis which maintains all behavior has a meaning and cause and that no behavior is arbitrary.

Rapprochment: A phase in early childhood development occurring approximately several months after the child's first birthday and lasting through the time of his or her second birthday. Due to the child's increasingly painful recognition that his or her mother is a separate and distinct entity, whose needs do not always coincide with his, the child actively seeks out the mother and behaves coercively toward her, in an effort to control her. Conflicts arise between the wish to remain one with the mother and the wish for autonomy.

Rationalization: A defense mechanism which functions to conceal unconscious unacceptable thoughts through the use of logical explanations.

Regression: A retreat to a less mature level of functioning. The regression may occur due to difficulty encountered at a later developmental level, or because of a fixation at an earlier level of development, due to unresolved conflicts.

Repression: A defense mechanism which functions to keep an idea, which would evoke anxiety, excluded from conscious awareness.

Separation: Initially, a process whereby a child gains an awareness of being distinct from its mother. This is in contrast to the state of oneness that is presumed, on the part of the infant in a symbiosis with its mother. Separation is regarded as a healthy developmental achievement.

Soothing Function: The ability to soothe oneself which derives from internalizing the soothing and reassuring qualities of one's mother in early childhood.

Symbiosis: The interdependency of mother and infant or a reference to that type of relationship, as in the complete interdependency of two people. Also referring to the infant's inferred experience of a state of oneness with its mother occurring between the sixth week of life through the first few months of life.

Subliminal: A stimulus that operates below the threshold of consciousness.

Sublimation: The unconscious conversion of sexual or aggressive behavior into behavior which is acceptable. For example, an infantile desire to express aggression by smearing feces on the wall, may be sublimated into a desire to paint, to smear paint on a canvas.

Superego: One of the three parts of the mind. The other two are the id and the ego. The superego maintains our ideals, values and prohibitions. The superego is commonly known as the conscience.

Symbolic: The representation of one thing by another.

Transitional object: This term first coined by Donald Winnicott, M.D., a pediatrician turned psychoanalyst, refers to the first "not-me" object the child treasures and uses to assuage the feeling of separation from mother. The child focuses on one object, which symbolizes both mother and child by virtue of its smells and touch.

True Self: A self which expresses one's actual beliefs and reality. This self is the child's innate potential and can survive only in a loving and emotionally healthy environment.

Unconscious: Those thoughts, feelings and impulses which are kept out of our conscious awareness in order to avoid anxiety.

Endnotes

1. James Coco and Marion Paone, *The James Coco Diet* (New York: Bantam Books, 1984), p. 12.

2. *ibid.*, p.13.

3. *Newsday*, May 18, 1996.

4. *ibid.*, May 4, 1993.

5. Robert Waldron, *Oprah!*, (New York: St. Martins Press, 1987).

6. Sigmund Freud, *A General Introduction to Psychoanalysis* (New York: Pocket Books, 1971), p. 305.

7. Charles Brenner, *An Elementary Textbook of Psychoanalysis* (New York: A Doubleday Anchor Book, 1957).

8. Sigmund Freud, *The Psychopathology of Everyday Life* (New York: W.W. Norton & Company, Inc., 1965).

9. Hilde Bruch, *The Importance of Overweight* (New York: W.W. Norton, 1957).

10. Margaret S. Mahler, *On the Current Status of the Infantile Neurosis, in The Selected Papers of Margaret S. Mahler, M.D.*, (New York and London: Jason Aronson, 1975).

11. Margaret S. Mahler credits analyst Phyllis Greenacre with the phrase "love affair with the world."

12. M. Sperling, "The Role of the Mother in Psychosomatic Disorders in Children," *Psychosomatic Medicine,* 11:377-385.

13. Anna Freud, "The Psychoanalytic Study of Infantile Feeding Disorders," in *Childhood Psychopathology,* ed. by S. Harrison and J. McDermitt (New York: International Universities Press, 1972).

14. Walter W. Hamburger, "The Occurrence and Meaning of Dreams of Food and Eating," *Psychosomatic Medicine*, XX (1958), p. 13.

15. Margaret S. Mahler, *The Selected Papers of Margaret S. Mahler, M.D.*

16. L. Silverman, F. Lachmann, and R. Milich, *The Search For Oneness,* (New York: International Universities Press, 1982).

17. *ibid.,* p. 100.

18. D.W. Winnicott, "Transitional Objects And Transitional Phenomena: A Study of the First Not-Me Possession," in *The International Journal of Psychoanalysis*, XXXLV, Part 2 (1953).

19. Robert Waldron, *Oprah!*, p. 138.

20. Renee Taylor, *My Life On A Diet, Confessions of a Hollywood Diet Junkie*, (New York: G. P. Putnam's Sons, 1986), p. 84.

21. Elizabeth Taylor, *Elizabeth Takes Off*, (Boston: G.K. Hall, 1989), p. 44.

22. Jacob A. Arlow, M.D., *Unconscious Fantasy*, (1969) in Psychoanalysis: *Clinical Theory and Practice,* (Connecticut: International Universities Press, 1991).

23. Sydney Smith, "The Golden Fantasy: A Regressive Reaction To Separation Anxiety," in *The International Journal of Psychoanalysis*, (1977) 58:311.

24. P. Benoit, P., O.P., "The Holy Eucharist," in *The Idea of Catholicism: An Introduction to the Thought and Worship of the Church*, ed. by Walter J. Burghardt, S.J., and William F. Lynch, S.J., (Cleveland and New York: The World Publishing Company), pp. 240-243.

25. W.J. Weatherby, *An Intimate Portrait of The Great One*, (New York: Pharos Books, 1992).

26. *Newsday*, January 23, 1996.

27. Elizabeth Taylor, *Elizabeth Takes Off*, p. 17.

28. *ibid*.

29. Marcia Millman, *Such A Pretty Face, Being Fat in America* (New York and London: W.W. Norton, 1980), p. 151.

30. *ibid*., p.73.

31. *ibid*., p. 85.

32. *ibid*., p. 182.

33. Otto Fenichel, *The Drive To Amass Wealth,* in *The Collected Papers of Otto Fenichel*, (New York: W.W. Norton, 1954), pp. 89-108.

34. Marcia Millman, *Such A Pretty Face, Being Fat in America.*

35. Harold I. Kaplan, M.D. and Helen Singer Kaplan, Ph.D., "The Psychosomatic Concept Of Obesity," in *Journal of Nervous and Mental Diseases*, (1956) 123:193.

36. Margaret Atwood, *Lady Oracle* (New York: Simon & Schuster, 1976).

37. Alice Miller, *Prisoners of Childhood* (New York: 1981).

38. Helene Deutsch, "Some Forms of Emotional Disturbance and Their Relationship to Schizophrenia," in *Psychoanalytic Quarterly*, (1942), 11:301-322.

39. Sophocles, "Oedipus Rex" in *Greek Tragedies Vol. 1*, ed. by David Grene and Richmond Lattimore, (Chicago: Chicago University Press, 1960).

40. Sigmund Freud, "The Interpretation of Dreams," (1900) in *The Standard Edition*, ed. by James Strachey, Vol. 19 (New York: Basic Books, 1956 by arrangement with George Allen & Unwin, Ltd. and the Hogarth Press, Ltd.), p. 296.

41. Sophocles, "Oedipus Rex" in *Greek Tragedies Vol. 1,* by David Grene and Richmond Lattimore, eds.

42. Robert Lindner, *The Fifty Minute Hour* (New Jersey: Jason Aronson, 1982).

43. *ibid.*, p. 115.

44. *ibid.*

45. *ibid.*

46. *ibid.*

47. *ibid.*, p. 134.

48. *ibid.*, p. 142.

49. *ibid.*, p. 166.

50. *ibid.*, p. 168.

51. Marcia Millman, *Such A Pretty Face, Being Fat in America*, p. 188.

52. Walter W. Hamburger, "The Occurrence and Meaning of Dreams of Food and Eating," *Psychosomatic Medicine.*

53. Harvey J. Schwartz, "Bulimia: Psychoanalytic Perspectives," in *Journal of the American Psychoanalytic Association*, (1958), p. 456.

54. Marcia Millman, *Such A Pretty Face, Being Fat in America*, p. 188.

55. Geneen Roth, *Feeding The Hungry Heart*, (Indianapolis and New York: The Bobbs-Merrill Co.,1982), p. 7.

56. *ibid.*, p. 8.

57. *ibid.*, p. 10.

58. Helmut Schoeck, Envy, *A Theory of Social Behavior* (New York: Harcourt, Brace & World, Inc., 1966).

59. Betsy Cohen, *The Snow White Syndrome, All About Envy* (New York: Macmillan Publishing Company, 1986).

60. *ibid.*

61. Clarence Maloney, ed., *The Evil Eye* (New York: Columbia University Press, 1976).

62. Betsy Cohen, The Snow White Syndrome, All About Envy, p. 49.

63. *ibid.*

64. *ibid.*

65. Copyright Home Box Office.

66. Helmut Schoeck, *Envy, A Theory of Social Behavior*, p. 107.

67. *ibid.*, p. 108.

68. *ibid.*, p. 109.

69. *ibid.*

70. Marcia Millman, *Such A Pretty Face, Being Fat in America*, p. 186.

71. Renee Taylor, *My Life On A Diet, Confessions of a Hollywood Diet Junkie*, p. 84.

72. Ann and Barry Ulanov, *Cinderella and Her Sisters, The Envied and the Envying* (Philadelphia: The Westminster Press, 1983), p. 21.

73. *ibid*.

74. Robert Waldron, *Oprah!*, p. 139.

75. Betsy Cohen, *The Snow White Syndrome: All About Envy*, p. 204.

76. Renee Taylor, *My Life On A Diet, Confessions of a Hollywood Diet Junkie*, p. 96.

77. Marcia Millman, *Such A Pretty Face, Being Fat in America*.

78. Gilles DeLeuze, *Masochism: An Interpretation of Coldness and Cruelty* (New York: George Braziller, Inc., Publishers, 1971).

79. *ibid*.

80. Jack Novick & Kerry Novick, "Some Comments on Masochism and Delusion of Omnipotence from a Developmental Perspective," in *Journal of the American Psychoanalytic Association*, Vol. 39, #2, pp. 307-31, 1991.

81. Ralph Greenson, "On Boredom" in *Journal of the American Psychoanalytic Association*, 1:7-21, 1953.

82. Meyer Mendelson, M.D., *Psychoanalytic Concepts of Depression*, 2nd edition, (New York: Spectrum Publications, 1974).

83. *ibid*.

84. *ibid*.

85. *ibid*.

86. Edith Jacobson, *Depression, Comparative Studies of Normal, Neurotic, and Psychotic Conditions*, (New York: International Universities Press, Inc., 1971).

87. Meyer Mendelson, M.D., *Psychoanalytic Concepts of Depression*.

88. Geneen Roth, *Feeding the Hungry Heart*, p. 19.

89. Roseanne Barr, *Roseanne, My Life As A Woman* (New York: Harper Collins Publishers, 1989), p. 10.

90. Myron L. Glucksman M.D. and Jules Hirsch, M.D. "The Response of Obese Patients to Weight Reduction," in *Psychosomatic Medicine*, XXXl, #1, 1969.

91. Myron L. Glucksman, M.D. and Jules Hirsch, M.D., "The Response of Obese Patients to Weight Reduction: A clinical Evaluation of Behavior," in *Psychosomatic Medicine*, XXX #1 1968.

92. Leonard Shengold, M.D., *Soul Murder*, (New Haven: Yale University Press, 1989).

93. Anthony Brandt, "I'm Not Half The Man I Used To Be," in *Forbes FYI* (New York: Forbes Inc. 1996), May 6, 1996, p. 108.

94. Colleen S.W. Rand, Ph.D., and Albert J. Stunkard, M.D., "Obesity and Psychoanalysis: Treatment and Four-Year Follow-Up," in *American Journal of Psychiatry*, 120:9, Sept., 1983.

Bibliography

Arlow, Jacob A., M.D., "Unconscious Fantasy" (1969). *Psychoanalysis: Clinical Theory and Practice*. Connecticut: International Universities Press, 1991.

Atwood, Margaret. *Lady Oracle*. New York: Simon & Schuster, 1976.

Barr, Roseanne. *Roseanne, My Life As A Woman*. New York: Harper Collins Publishers, 1989.

Benoit, P., O.P., "The Holy Eucharist" T*he Idea of Catholicism: An Introduction to the Thought and Worship of the Church*. edited by Walter J. Burghardt, S.J. and William F. Lynch, S.J. Cleveland and New York: The World Publishing Company.

Brandt, Anthony. "I'm Not Half The Man I Used To Be." *Forbes FYI*, May 6, 1996, p.108.

Brenner, Charles, M.D. *An Elementary Textbook of Psychoanalysis*. New York: A Doubleday Anchor Book, 1957.

Brenner, Charles, M.D. *The Mind in Conflict*. New York: International Universities Press, Inc., 1982.

Bruch, Hilde. *The Importance of Overweight*. New York: W. W. Norton, 1957.

Coco, James and Paone, Marion. *The James Coco Diet*. New York: Bantam Books, 1984.

Cohen, Betsy. *The Snow White Syndrome: All About Envy*. New York: Macmillan Publishing Company, 1986.

DeLeuze, Gilles. *Masochism: An Interpretation of Coldness and Cruelty*. New York: George Braziller, Inc. Publishers, 1971.

Deutsch, Helene. "Some Forms of Emotional Disturbance and Their Relationship to Schizophrenia." *Psychoanalytic Quarterly*. (1942), 11:301-322.

Edward, Joyce; Ruskin, Nathene; and Turrini, Patsy. *Separation/Individuation Theory and Application*. 2nd ed. New York, London, Sydney: Gardner Press, Inc., 1991.

Erikson, Erik H. *Identity, Youth and Crisis*. New York: W.W. Norton & Company, Inc., 1968.

Fenichel, Otto. "The Drive To Amass Wealth." *The Collected Papers of Otto Fenichel*. New York: W.W. Norton, 1954.

Freud, Anna. *The Ego and the Mechanisms of Defense*. Vol. II of The Writings of Anna Freud. Revised Edition. New York: International Universities Press, Inc., 1966.

Freud, Anna. "The Psychoanalytic Study of Infantile Feeding Disorders." *Childhood Psychopathology*, edited by S. Harrison and J. McDermitt. New York: International Universities Press, 1972.

Freud, Sigmund. *The Interpretation of Dreams*. (1900) Vol.19 of *The Standard Edition*. Edited by James Strachey. New York: Basic Books, 1956 by arrangement with George Allen & Unwin, Ltd. and the Hogarth Press, Ltd.

Freud, Sigmund. *The Psychopathology of Everyday Life*. New York: W.W. Norton & Company, Inc., 1965.

Freud, Sigmund. *A General Introduction to Psychoanalysis*. New York: Pocket Books, 1971.

Glucksman, Myron L., M.D., and Hirsch, Jules, M.D. "The Response of Obese Patients to Weight Reduction," *Psychosomatic Medicine* XXXl, No. 1, (1969).

Greenson, Ralph. *Explorations in Psychoanalysis*. New York: International Universities Press, Inc., 1978.

Greenson, Ralph. "On Boredom." *Journal of the American Psychoanalytic Association*, 1:7-21, (1953).

Hamburger, Walter W. "The Occurrence and Meaning of Dreams of Food and Eating." *Psychosomatic Medicine.* XX (1958).

Home Box Office.

Jacobson, Edith, M.D. *Depression, Comparative Studies of Normal, Neurotic, and Psychotic Conditions*. New York: International Universities Press, Inc.,1971.

Jacobson, Edith, M.D. *The Self and the Object World*. New York: International Universities Press, Inc., 1964.

Johnson, Craig, and Connors, Mary E. *The Etiology and Treatment of Bulimia Nervosa, A Biopsychosocial Perspective*. New York: Basic Books, 1950.

Kaplan, Harold I., M.D., and Kaplan, Helen Singer, Ph.D. "The Psychosomatic Concept Of Obesity." *Journal of Nervous and Mental Diseases.* (1956) 123:193.

Kernberg, Otto, M.D. *Object Relations Theory and Clinical Psychoanalysis*. New York: Jason Aronson, Inc., 1976.

Lindner, Robert. *The Fifty Minute Hour* New Jersey: Jason Aronson, 1982.

Mahler, Margaret S. *On the Current Status of the Infantile Neurosis. The Selected Papers of Margaret S. Mahler, M.D.* New York and London: Jason Aronson, 1975.

Maloney, Clarence, ed. *The Evil Eye*. New York: Columbia University Press, 1976.

Mendelson, Meyer M.D., *Psychoanalytic Concepts of Depression*, 2nd edition, (New York: Spectrum Publications, 1974).

Miller, Alice. *Prisoners of Childhood.* New York: 1981.

Millman, Marcia. *Such A Pretty Face, Being Fat in America.* New York and London: W. W. Norton and Co., 1980.

Moore, Burness E., M.D., and Fine, Bernard D., M.D. *Psychoanalytic Terms and Concepts.* New Haven and London: Psychoanalytic Association and Yale University Press, 1990.

Newsday. January 23, 1996.

Newsday, May 4, 1996

Newsday. May 18, 1996.

Novick, Jack, and Novick, Kerry. "Some Comments on Masochism and Delusion of Omnipotence from a Developmental Perspective." *Journal of the American Psychoanalytic Association,* 39, No.2:307-31, (1991).

Rand, Colleen, S.W. Ph.D., and Stunkard, Albert J., M.D. "Obesity and Psychoanalysis: Treatment and Four-Year Follow-Up." *American Journal of Psychiatry.* 120:9, (September, 1983).

Roth, Geneen. Feeding *The Hungry Heart*. Indianapolis and New York: The Bobbs-Merrill Co., 1982.

Schoeck, Helmut. Envy, *A Theory of Social Behavior.* New York: Harcourt, Brace & World, Inc.,1966.

Schwartz, Harvey J. "Bulimia: Psychoanalytic Perspectives." *Journal of the American Psychoanalytic Association.* (1958).

Shengold, Leonard, M.D. *Soul Murder*. New Haven: Yale University Press, 1989.

Silverman, L., Lachmann, F., and Milich, R. *The Search For Oneness*. New York: International Universities Press, 1982.

Smith, Sydney. "The Golden Fantasy: A Regressive Reaction To Separation Anxiety" *The International Journal of Psychoanalysis*. (1977) 58:311.

Sophocles, *Oedipus Rex*. Vol. 1 of *Greek Tragedies*. Edited by David Grene and Richmond Lattimore. Chicago: Chicago University Press, 1960.

Sperling, M. "The Role of the Mother in Psychosomatic Disorders in Children." *Psychosomatic Medicine*. 11:377-385.

Taylor, Elizabeth. *Elizabeth Takes Off*. Boston: G.K. Hall 1989.

Taylor, Renee. *My Life On A Diet, Confessions of a Hollywood Diet Junkie*. New York: G. P. Putnam's Sons, 1986.

Ulanov, Ann and Barry. *Cinderella and Her Sisters, The Envied and the Envying*. Philadelphia: The Westminster Press, 1983.

Waldron, Robert. *Oprah!*. New York: St. Martins Press, 1987.

Weatherby, W.J. *An Intimate Portrait of The Great One*. New York: Pharos Books, 1992.

Wilson, C. Philip, M.D., ed. With assistance of Hogan, Charles C., M.D., and Mintz, Ira L., M.D. *Fear of Being Fat, The Treatment of Anorexia Nervosa and Bulimia*. Revised Edition. New Jersey and London: Jason Aronson, Inc., 1985.

Winnicott, D.W. "Transitional Objects And Transitional Phenomena: A Study of the First Not-Me Possession." *The International Journal of Psychoanalysis*. XXXLV, Part 2, (1953).

Index